W0009269

Mother
Daze

Tales from the Imperfect Playground

Christine Carr

PublishingWorks, Inc.
151 Epping Rd.
Exeter, NH 03833
603-778-9883
www.publishingworks.com

For Sales and Orders:
1-800-738-6603 or 603-772-7200

Designed by Kat Mack

LCCN: 2009920801
ISBN-10: 1-933002-85-9
ISBN-13: 978-1-933002-85-9

Mother
Daze

Dedication

This book is dedicated to my mother,
Mary Jane (Millard) Boucher—my very first friend.

Table of Contents

Letter to My Children
by Joy Veaudry

If I do not see
all the early turnings of your life,
if I am not here
to applaud your risings
and to offer my shoulders
as ground for your tears
when success eludes you
or when sorrow visits
as it must
in its season,
if I am only memory
when your hand
reaches for the phone
and you stop,
realizing
I will no longer answer—
know that as you woke into being
I breathed into you
the full energy of my heart,
every wish and hope and dream,
enough love to last
your whole life long.
That gift sleeps within you,
a blessing to wake and caress you
if you need me
and I am gone.

Foreword

Nothing means more to me than my two children, Sarah and Matthew. Motherhood, on the other hand, is a different story completely. Loving my children and motherhood bring different (and some days opposite) emotions.

We see so many mothers all our lives and dream of how we'll be as mothers so often growing up that it really should be easier than that incredible uncertainty and fear that invades us through pregnancy and catapults itself front and center on that ride to the delivery room. And who among us would think during the throes of labor and nervous hopes for a healthy child that the day would turn out to be the best day of our lives? But for all the trepidation, the self-doubt, and the incredible inhumanity of legs in stirrups and fingers clenched firmly around the throat of the man we suspended any love for, comes something so wonderful, so innocent, and so all-ours that we are quite sure, maybe for the first time ever, that we understand true love. As mothers, we are imbued with a primal will to do anything to protect, nurture, and adore God's greatest gift.

Yet how quickly time moves those adoring eyes of our precious infant into orbs rolling in our teenager's head at the simple request to pick up the four days' worth of underwear lying in his room. But have I ever seen a more beautiful girl than my daughter up there on stage; a boy more loyal and true than my son who just yesterday wouldn't take out the garbage but is now carrying in all the groceries in a downpour just so I don't have to?

If you're like me, and I hope you are, you're blessed (or about to be) with wonderfully imperfect children. We appreciate them for who they are and not what we hope or want them to be. We've made so many mistakes and done or said so many things we wish we could take back in raising them; but through it all, there they are, our singular and constant reminder of why we were born and how we've been called to play a part in God's greatest miracle. What an awesome responsibility; what an awesome gift.

Best,
Doris Burke,
ESPN Basketball Commentator

Acknowledgments

From the moment I first put pen to paper, I knew something very special was happening. *Mother Daze* gushed out from my heart in order to spread a message I thought women could comfortably embrace. This book is a celebration. As such, it is only fitting that before we can begin, I must offer up a toast of thanks to a number of remarkable individuals that helped throughout this process. It's so gratifying to recognize and honor such a terrifically talented group of people. You can bet your boots I am fortunate to be surrounded by this true team of champions!

First and foremost, there would be no story without my three little loves: Nolan, Jane, and Finley. Those magical birds will never fully grasp how much happiness they have brought into my life. I am blessed, even amongst the chaos! Although they have certainly tested my patience, luckily they always manage to rally back with some sort of comic relief. How quickly the displeasures of a day can be erased with a comment like, "Memember (remember) Mommy, at fourteen o'clock I am going to give you one hundred kisses and nine hugs." It is my hope that those three cuties continue to brighten the world around them while they joyfully lead their lives.

Furthermore, I owe a humongous hug of gratitude to my husband Andy. His never-ending love, continued kindness, and active role in parenting our children do not go unnoticed. To share this life with someone so sincere is a treat.

Undeniably, I am thankful for my parents, Mary Jane and David Boucher, and my two sisters, Sharon and Bethany. Those four people have created an invaluable sense of home that has followed me throughout my life. They have shaped my soul, and for that I am ever grateful.

Additionally, I am filled with an overabundance of appreciation for Jeremy Townsend, my editor and Supreme Literary Goddess. Her willingness to give me a chance is unforgettable. Her wit and wisdom are delightful qualities that make her so enjoyable to work with. As a matter of fact, the entire Publishing Works crew deserves a rowdy round of applause, especially Carol Corbett, Kieran Haseler, and Kat Mack.

Recognizing my dear friend Sandra K. Basile, author of *A Mother's Circle*, is an honor. She was such a key player throughout the entire writing process. Her undeniable knowledge, on-target advice, and honest opinions granted me the courage to make this book fly.

It is without question that the extremely talented and generous Doris Burke holds a special place in my heart. I am grateful for her eagerness to pen the foreword, the overall graciousness and dependability she exudes, and the active interest she had in this story.

Not to forget Marc Blevins, friend and author of *Pray for the Dead*, who offered such instant availability and continued confidence. His belief in this project was impressive.

The award-winning photographer Michelle Carr lent her genius eye and captured the picture that is displayed on the cover of this book. I am grateful for her talented vision.

Many thanks go out to my technical support team of Donna Hayes and Joel Evans of Geek.com. During the various stages of development, they each provided many long hours of labor. I am not exactly a technical genius, but with their help, I could at least pretend to be one.

I must also send out a bugle blast of thanks to Chad Verdi, Dan Doyle, Carolyn Thornton, Mary Egan-Callahan, Patrick Wholey, and Betty Jo Cotter, who have all provided key advice and assurance that enabled me to tap into my true potential as a writer.

To continue this testimonial of appreciation, my "test readers" merit a standing ovation, for sure. Each of these busy individuals nestled in to read my original manuscript and challenged me to write the best book possible. With their trusted hints and suggestions, I was able to fine-tune the message and clarify my intent: Mary Jane Boucher, Sharon Boucher, Bethany Boucher, Kristin Dyer, Svetlana Levin, Donna Evans, Kathleen Lalonde, Michael Lalonde, Dana Haxton, Meaghan Carty, Cindy Hagerty, Lindsay Daskalopoulos, Kengy Bell, and Sherri Coale (Oklahoma Sooners Basketball Coach).

I want to give a special acknowledgment to Joy Veaudry. The moment I read her poem, "Letter to My Children," I knew it was a perfect fit for this book. I am pleased that the Olney Street Press allowed it to be connected to my story. You can find more beautiful poetry in her book, *A Clear Path Home*, which was published in 2008.

And last, but certainly not least, I want to recognize the thousands of children I have been able to teach throughout my physical education career at Frenchtown Elementary School. Those kids have taught me, time and time again, the beautiful magic associated with childhood innocence and youthful simplicity.

I'm Jumping In:
An Introduction

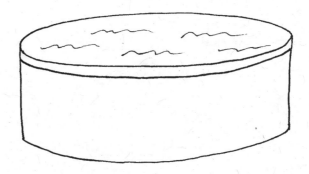

February 23—the day the hypothetical lightning bolt un-expectedly struck and I jumped head first into the concept of putting pen to paper. It was chilly that afternoon, as I bustled into the grocery store. School vacation was in full swing and I was in need of some last-minute supplies for a family getaway to Cape Cod, Massachusetts. At the time, our three young children—Nolan (age six), Jane (age three), and Finley (seventeen months)—were excited about the excursion.

While waiting at the deli counter, I stood next to a young mother and her child. The little girl smiled at me, so I commented on how adorable she was and asked the typical question, "How old is she?"

"She's eleven months old," her mother responded.

"She's quite friendly."

The mother agreed. "She seems pretty sociable and very well adjusted." I questioned whether or not she had started to crawl. She explained that her daughter was beginning to get herself into a bit of mischief. I offered, "That sure is an exhausting stage." She countered with, "No, I really love it! It's everything I had expected and more." While we continued to wait, I mentioned that I was a Physical Education teacher at a public elementary school and the woman thought that was interesting. "Oh, wow! She'll probably attend a public school one day, but may need a more structured environment provided in a private school setting. She's quite coordinated and seems to work well with others at play dates. We are attending a gymnastics class once a week, swim class on Mondays at the YMCA, and enjoying a music class in Providence on Tuesdays." I was amused, yet honestly quite stunned. My three-year-old daughter had yet to see the likes of a gymnastics studio, never mind my seventeen-month-old.

Anyway, my number was finally called, the deli order was filled, and I said goodbye to the young mother. As I raced swiftly through the aisles like an ostrich, I couldn't help but review the details of that brief conversation in my head. Have we mothers gone mad? The child was eleven months old . . . private school or public? Involved in three activities? Then I realized, unfortunately, nowadays it's not uncommon for women to feel an endless pull towards enrichment activities for their kids.

After quickly checking out at the register, I returned back home, ran in and gathered the luggage, snacks, juice boxes, diapers, and wipes, then began to load the car. My husband, Andy, was inside with the kids, as I checked and re-checked the to-do list. We were only staying for two nights, but I nevertheless felt compelled to pack the entire house.

As I corralled my three kids to the car, Jane was complaining that Nolan was in her seat and Finley was already requesting a drink. We hadn't even rolled out of the driveway and my chest was already beginning to tighten. Ah, family fun. To add fuel to this fire, I had to call to my Prince Charming twice to hurry up as he scoured the last few pages of the newspaper while slowly sauntering like a basset hound towards our car. (In the eighteen years that I've known him, Andy has often struggled with the concept of time. Before we got married it was worse, but much to his credit, it has improved . . . a bit!)

While we cruised up I-95 North, Andy was annoyed with my directions. He did not think I was delivering the exit numbers fast enough and questioned the actual route we were taking. But let me think: Did he have any interest in mapping out the itinerary beforehand? No, that would have been too difficult; however, critiquing it now was quite easy. Instead of feeding into my escalating urge to mimic a WWE SmackDown, I sat quietly with my thoughts.

As the car pressed on, I continued to reflect on the mother's comments in the grocery store. Although she was smiling and seemed happy, she looked a bit overwhelmed as she listed the weekly details of her mother-daughter routine, as if what she was doing had been expected in order to be considered a "good mom." I think the words, "I really love it! It's everything I expected and more!" were really a secret code translation for, "Help me! I'm freakin' tired!" Her double-eye blink mixed with a subtle head twitch was a dead giveaway.

It was at that moment, while driving in the car, that I decided to write. I began to reflect on all of the women in my life, how impressive each one is, and how much we miraculously get done. My thoughts jumped from beach excursions to birthday parties, from friendships to family history. While my three children took turns complaining in the backseat, I gazed forward and smiled. I became oddly excited. I actually laughed out loud. Andy casually glanced my way, but didn't pick up on it, so I enjoyed the inside jolly with myself.

I imagined how glorious women are amid the humor, sorrow, love, and laughter. I recalled my dear friend who sat with me in the emergency room for four hours after I had been involved in a minor car accident. I remembered the mother at the local Super Center who tried to restrain her tantruming child as he jiggled like a bucking-bronco in her arms, and I visualized that first-time mom crying in the pediatrician's office because her infant wouldn't eat. I thought about the tired co-worker who was caring for her aging mother because her brother just *wasn't* available, and a single mother who was struggling to pay her bills. Time and time again, I found myself repeating the same words in my head: "We women are great . . . We women are great!" We magically do it all, yet never quite think we've accomplished enough.

This book is a tribute in the truest sense of the word, and it is my hope that you perceive it as such. I do not pretend to have the answers, nor do I claim to have this parenthood thing all figured out. I am not asking the women of the world to burn their bras at the local Village Green, and I certainly do not conceal a superhero suit of spandex underneath my clothes—although sporting a girdle of yesteryear would be quite beneficial after an occasional daylong binge. Nonetheless, while viewing the front cover photo of the latest celebrity mom baring her six-pack abs and a headline reading, "Lose 20 pounds in 20 minutes," I am reminded of the insanity we face as women in today's society. On any given day, my own abdominal region resembles a wad of pizza dough waiting to rise, so I see it as unfair that society unrealistically expects us to be that skinny-assed wonder woman who maintains a level of perfection in every aspect of her life. I'm all for raising the bar, but how high is too high?

Parenting is definitely a work in progress, but when did everything become so serious? *Do I get my two-year-old the toy that speaks in Spanish and French or just the one that introduces the map of the United States?* Hola, we're talking about a two-year-old; whatever happened to colors, shapes, and the occasional nursery rhyme? *Have I given enough to charity? Am I reading the right books with my kids? Are those mathematical flash cards appropriate? Should I get him a tutor? Can I be more involved? Shall we go to the zoo or the aquarium?* The calculated craziness needs to stop! Instead of the endless questioning, look at how terrific our kids are and consider it a direct link to our parenting. Unless, of course, the behaviors are somewhat undesirable, then that's where the paternal side of the family kicks in. (Kidding!)

There's no doubt this road trip through life will have its fair share of pot holes, skid marks, and setbacks. I never can tell what will be waiting around the next corner. There is no MapQuest available to guide me, and the characters I will meet along the

trails are yet to be determined. There will always be situations that test my patience, but I do try to search for that break in the clouds. Case in point, the family trip to Cape Cod was a bit nerve-wracking, but it did provide the spark that inspired me to write this tale.

Somewhere along the way, I think we have lost touch with the realities of raising young kids. This high-octane parenting is exhausting and it needs to be revisited. Like any good policy, it's important to assess the situation and recognize if things need to be changed. These days, most folks are trying desperately to shield their families from every dysfunction, dilemma, and disaster—well-intentioned and certainly necessary. However, I think it's gone too far. Protection is one thing, but duct taping them to our leg is a little too much.

This book is a wake-up call to take action in our own world. Spread the word. We need to start recognizing the comedy, give ourselves some credit, and above all, laugh at the ridiculousness of life. My sister Beth said it best: "People like to hear other people's stuff." So, at the ripe old age of thirty-seven, here is my "stuff." As I attempt to take the plunge with every bump and bruise exposed, my hope is that you are right alongside, testing the water to see if it's safe enough to come in. Cannonball!

1.
Heavy with Child . . . Literally!

Summer 1999. It had been thirty-nine days since my last menstrual cycle. It was a Saturday morning. Andy had already left for the day and I was lying in bed watching the *Weekend Today* show. Those were the days when I could actually "sleep in," and then comfortably lounge under the covers just clicking aimlessly from one channel to the next. Damn, I never appreciated the full value of that opportunity. When I eventually got up to use the bathroom, much to my surprise, there was still no monthly visitor. A bit nervous, I decided it was time to purchase a pregnancy test kit. I had never bought one before, and I was embarrassed. I didn't want to bump into anyone doing their weekend shopping, so I traveled ten minutes to a less-populated pharmacy in order to make my purchase. God forbid anyone familiar should spot me.

Walking into the store, I tried to be inconspicuous as I headed toward *the* aisle. From a safe distance, I glanced at each box trying to figure out which test kit was best. I actually felt weird buying it, as if people were watching me. I had a vision of a giant spotlight beaming down on my head. I imagined a deep voice chiming in over the PA system, "Attention all shoppers, the young lady in aisle three thinks she is pregnant. I repeat, the blonde girl pretending *not* to look at the kits could in fact be having a baby . . ."

One of the test kits came as a two pack, buy one get one free, so I jumped at the bargain and made my way to the register. I was slightly embarrassed to place the box on the counter, so I tried to mix it in with a loaf of bread, a pack of gum, and a roll of paper towels. Wasn't I tricky? Oddly enough, I felt compelled to explain myself to the worker donning a smock peppered with pins of dachshund puppies, white kittens, and one large button of Conway Twitty. "Warm day out there," I attempted. The stoic cashier mumbled back, "Yep," while she continued to ring up my order. Obviously having no appetite for small talk, I caught her roaming retinas scanning for something gold and sparkly wrapped around my left appendage while she placed the pregnancy kit in the bag. As I reached for my purse, I made sure that my wedding ring was in full view. Ridiculously, I wanted her to know that I was not involved in some torrid affair in which I now had to "pay the piper" for my risqué behavior. Meanwhile, the older woman probably enjoyed her own inner giggle recognizing that, if in fact the test proved positive, my entire world would be rocked in a matter of months.

After bravely making the purchase, I drove home and immediately ran to the bathroom. I must have read the foolproof directions four times. Seriously, how can someone goof it up? Yet, I didn't want to leave any chance for error. Once I completed the procedure, I waited five minutes (not a second earlier), paced back and forth, went upstairs, downstairs, and then lumbered back to "the stick." As soon as I walked into the bathroom, I spotted it—one pink line right through the middle. I immediately grabbed the box to review the diagram. Yes, it was true, I indeed was pregnant. Yahoo!

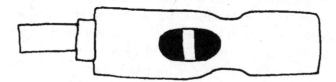

From that day forward, I've never looked back. I remember telling Andy as soon as he came home. He was thrilled! I called my doctor to schedule an appointment. And with that, the adventure began.

Mothers all recall those joyful days of pregnancy, when our belly skin is stretched to maximum capacity, our "cankles" resemble tree trunks, and varicose veins rage up and down our legs. I was horrified to witness what was happening to my body while heavy with child—an absolute science project just waiting to burst. The ability to breathe normally became a daily test and the possibility for a good night's sleep was out of the question.

I've heard many women boast, "I loved being pregnant!" Liars. Accomplishing those nine months (ten months actually) is a feat in itself. No doubt, seeing that pink line appear on the test strip released an intense connection and an immediate hold on my heart. However, while my waistline expanded and morning sickness carried on into the evening, I discovered that pregnancy was a monumental ordeal!

I absolutely loved the end result, but the process by which we got there always threw me for a loop. Blood tests and the waiting game for all of the results was enough to send me right over the edge. And the doctor's appointments spent sitting awkwardly on an examining table, clothed in a gown that exposed my entire naked backside were equally intimidating. Not to mention the paper placed beneath me that crinkled when I fidgeted. I would sit completely still and wait for the exam while staring at models of vaginas and posters of fallopian tubes displayed on the walls. During my first pregnancy, I worried about my own nutrition, Lamaze classes, exercise requirements (and limitations), and marveled at just how "gigantor" my belly actually could get. The health of the baby growing inside was a constant concern—not to be dwelled on, but certainly never far from my thoughts. Each person I bumped into was always ready to offer up a few tips: classical music in utero, lie on your left side, rub cocoa oil on your belly to avoid stretch marks (regrettably, my friends "Ben and Jerry" foiled any hopes of that plan ever working). The suggestions were never-ending and indeed well-intentioned. "You look good," people would lie. "I can't even tell you are pregnant." Yeah, right, as I jiggled my neck fat with fingers as thick as Jimmy Dean sausage links. So does that mean I normally look forty pounds overweight? Great!

Thanks to a couple of baby showers, I had all of the necessary gear I would never need. I recall the hours spent at the baby store con-scientiously trying to find the best matching unisex fabric pattern for the car seat, high chair, and pack n' play. Name books were carefully reviewed, BabyCenter.com was continuously explored, and Dreft was being bought and stockpiled for future loads of laundry.

I remember reading the important reasons for not carrying or lifting heavy objects. I followed those rules religiously. Sometimes I questioned whether or not my own pocketbook may have exceeded the proper weight limit. Flash forward to pregnancy numbers two and three, not only was I carrying the twenty-pound sibling, I was now hoisting the fifteen-pound diaper bag, as well as my pocketbook, all while balancing a cup of coffee on top of my head. Oh yes, how about that caffeine? Caffeine was not allowed with pregnancy number one, but somehow during the following pregnancies that rule was forgotten.

During my second pregnancy, I underwent an amniocentesis. I had received a false positive on the AFP (alpha-fetoprotein) test that is given during the fifteenth and twentieth week of gestation, in order to detect fetal abnormalities. Considering my results, it was recommended that I have an amnio done. I must admit, when I saw a needle the length of a yard stick coming my way, I was concerned. Yet, for someone who gets rather spooked by medical procedures, the encounter was not too bad and, hallelujah, my baby was going to be just fine. As dicey as that scene was, the real scare came after my third child was born. The delivery had gone off without a hitch and I thought I was home free . . . Wrong! Ah, foiled again. Shortly after her Apgar scores were tallied, I developed an incredible headache. At first, I thought it was par for the course. Having just given birth, one expects to have some aftershocks, but this was different... very different! The medical staff determined that I had a spinal headache due to the fact that the anesthesiologist had punctured the dura (a membrane surrounding the brain and spinal cord that seals in the spinal fluid). The experience was horrifying. Four days had passed and I still could not lift my head without feeling as if it might explode. That's awesome with a newborn, a two-year-old, and a five-year-old to care for. The scariest part of all was I didn't know if the pain would ever go away. *Was there nerve damage? Would I have to live with a chronic condition?* It was an unsettling state of mind. Eventually after two "blood patch" procedures (delightful term), the headache was gone and I was back to normal again—if that is even possible with three children.

In addition to my own silly stories, many friends have experienced some classic pregnancy adventures over the years as well: seven months of bed rest, a gall bladder bursting three days before delivery, twenty-four-hour labors, emergency c-sections, and an epidural that made one friend's legs feel disconnected from her body. Yet, remarkably we all manage to remove the alarming stories from the memory bank, thus allowing us the insanity of doing it again and again. A friend of mine actually claimed she couldn't wait for her scheduled c-section. She already had two children and therefore looked forward to a few days of rest at the hospital. Imagine that, choosing surgical pains over parental pains. For me, however, I was always completely thrilled when the ten-month condition was over. To be able to breathe freely and know that I had given birth to a little person was the best!

To think, it all starts from those unpredictable stages of pregnancy. Before that first happy hug was even shared, I felt that overwhelming attraction to each little dumpling. With all of my pregnancy anxieties and obvious discomforts aside, I couldn't wait to see each baby face. I try to awaken the joy I felt after every ultrasound; seeing that x-ray image of a tiny child growing inside was exciting. What a treat to lend my love to three individuals.

Long before the nap schedules, play dates, and homework horrors, I waited in a bathroom staring at a stick, hoping to see the "all-telling" pink line. I am confident that parenthood will provide the greatest pleasure in my life and remain my most valued accomplishment. So whatever I went through to get there was worth every ache, pain, moan, and groan. To be able to nurture a little person through life is a blessing—a complete, incomparable miracle.

2.
Brand-New Territory

Saturday, May 6—Nolan Andrew Carr arrives. After months of anticipation and thirty-six hours of labor, he was finally here. It was love at first sight once that swaddled little bunny was placed in my arms. He was nine pounds of pure sweetness. Nonetheless, I hadn't even finished my last cup of ice chips, nor had I been unhooked from my IV drip, and it was already time to give this tiny tot some food. As my due date had closed in, the more I read, the more I felt compelled to at least give breast-feeding a try. I was a bit squeamish about nursing, but everything I read described the experience as something so wonderful, so natural and free—an important way to bond with your baby, and not to mention, very convenient. Somehow the subjects of engorgement, high fevers, clogged ducts, or weaning nightmares didn't come up. And a "latch-on" comparable to the bite-down of a bear trap was somehow left out of the descriptions as well. It's interesting how such details get overlooked.

I can still taste the tears that were rolling down my cheeks after the lactation nurse assured me, "We'll just keep on trying, every hour, all day long . . . we'll get him on." As we wrestled with various positioning options and techniques, I questioned how this glorious birth had now become so clouded with anxiety? It was the moment I knew I had crossed over into brand-new territory. Could I call my mother?

That first night, Nolan slept in the nursery at the hospital. Andy and I were afraid that something might happen and, being utterly exhausted, we would not wake to the sounds of his distress. I recall the sound of the squeaky wheels on the moveable bassinet as the nurse rolled Nolan into my room for the 3:00 a.m. feeding. Welcome to motherhood! It still gives me goose bumps (better yet, scary chills) because it symbolized such an absolute change to my existence. It was as if my husband and I had been catapulted into adulthood, launched away from the somewhat carefree lifestyle we had been living, now replaced by a world of new challenges and much less sleep.

After spending two days in the safety of the hospital, it was time to check out and begin this adventure on our own. Before we could do that, a nurse came to the room and gave us a ten-minute pop-quiz on infant care and procedures. She asked questions about diapering, bathing, feeding, cord care, nail clipping, and then instructed us not to have "intimate relations" for three weeks. I gasped! Are you kidding me? What type of sadistic Samaritan suggests that? Three weeks? Try three years. After what I just experienced, that area was closed *indefinitely!* Did she forget I was wearing a foot-long maxi pad as thick as a mattress between my legs? Hell, I felt like I was back at my old job making sandwiches each time I layered the three Tucks pads and one squeeze of Lanacane cream on top of that cotton monstrosity.

On the drive home from the hospital, I sat in the back seat, just staring into Nolan's precious eyes. We listened to the *Phantom of the Opera* CD, and the beautiful voices, coupled with my delicate emotions, made me weep. Meanwhile, Andy transformed his driving abilities to that of a ninety-year-old woman. He crawled along at forty-five miles per hour on the highway, and most likely would have preferred to be driving an armored tank rather than our SUV. We should have been traveling in the breakdown lane because even in the "slow lane" we were driving too cautiously. A neon sign blinking, "Don't Come within Eighty Feet of This Vehicle: Crowned Prince on Board," would have been beneficial.

Our first two nights home from the hospital, we had back-to-back thunderstorms and lost power during the nighttime hours. That's handy for pre-dawn feedings! When my milk had finally "come in," Nolan could not figure out how to latch-on. How could he? My breasts looked as though a full gallon of silicone had been injected into each one. Holy Debbie does Dallas! All I needed was Andy to be clothed in silk jammies donning a captain's hat and we would have made quite the bawdy pair. Where were the reality chapters on that? As my husband scurried to figure out the directions to the manual breast pump, I distinctly remember my piercing question, "Who the hell am I? Friggin' Martha Washington?" as the crying from my newborn permeated the room and we struggled by candlelight to get him to eat. Well, needless to say, the start of a new day brought sunshine and soon we began to understand the massive life change we had embarked on. As connections were being made and the feeding system got easier, that little muffin crept deeper into my heart.

That first year as Mommy, I quite possibly experienced every emotion. Love for a new child, loss of the personal freedom to come and go as I pleased, doubt as to whether or not I knew what the heck I was doing, exhaustion, sadness, and lots of enjoyment. You name it, I felt it. To be temporarily disconnected from the land of the living is not easy. Such promise an infant brings, but three hours of sleep and round-the-clock feedings can surely mess with a woman's head. When all of the adoring visitors call it a night and venture home to bed, the new mother is faced with the reality that her night shift with a newborn is just getting started.

Springtime has always been referred to as a rebirth. How fitting, because I do believe I walked into my own sort of rebirth that day in May. The life I knew before children will never be back. The days when I could pick up and go, worry free, are gone. The constant concerns and endless cycle of feeding, diapering, feeding, diapering became my new reality. Whenever I see a new mother, I think back to those early days of parenting. I recall the hours spent virtually paralyzed by a breast pump eagerly awaiting my next Sitz bath. I remember questioning whether or not I would ever turn on the stove and actually cook a meal again, or if in fact Oreos were now considered an acceptable option for a dinner entrée.

And how about the careless people of the world that remark such silly comments like, "Oh, just wait. This is the easy phase," when talking about a small baby. Where do these senseless birdbrains come from? It most certainly is not such a cinch for the woman in charge. I was at a birthday party once for one of my son's friends. As I spoke with the child's grandmother, she told me that she had five children and remarked, "God was good to me. If only they could have stayed young." I wondered if nostalgic Granny was singing that same song while child rearing those five through the infant, toddler, and teen years. Hindsight is 20/20, but when we're in those beginning stages of parenting, often we're as blind as a drunken sailor.

Truth be told, most of the irritating experiences of baby number one were *not* present for babies two and three because the inexperience and uncertainty were gone. I was not as emotionally fragile. I had the advantage of recognizing that time does go by and, surprisingly enough, we learn to figure out what the hell to do. As a matter of fact, Dreft detergent was never bought again, the matching car seat pattern was no longer important, and we were certainly not listening to Broadway show tunes while crawling home in the slow lane with babies number two and three. Instead, we zipped along in the fast lane, anxious to simply get home.

However, when we're new at parenting, it's a challenge. That is precisely why we must remain a team—husband, in-laws, family, and friends. Everyone needs to be supportive of that new mom . . . unless they want to witness a Linda Blair look-alike competition. Don't forget how truly difficult those first few months as a rookie mother really were. New moms are sensitive creatures and must be treated as such, so we should always proceed with caution as they try to figure out their brand-new territory.

3.
The Mental F-Bomb

Boy, for someone who very rarely swears, I've adopted a few favorites that provide quite a nice release while parenting my three children. I love my kids more than anything, but let's all admit it, the job of motherhood is the toughest job there is, hands down! I have always had an infinite amount of patience when dealing with the people in the world around me, and as a P.E. teacher I have the opportunity to cheerfully entertain children on a daily basis. How is it, though, that my own three little ones are not as enchanted by my shtick?

Somehow I got through the books on pregnancy and "What to do the first year," but, regrettably, I was never told what to do when *all else fails*. Everything about motherhood was made to look so peaceful and fresh in these books. Anger and frustration were rarely discussed. Complete and utter exhaustion may have been mentioned, but somehow lists of appropriate swear words must have been misplaced. Without a doubt, there are parenting moments when all the appropriate coping mechanisms shut down and a list of the most offensive phrases would be mentally beneficial—not necessarily to be said out loud, but rather expressed humorously in my mind. When the acknowledgment is made that I may possibly grind away every last tooth in my mouth (by clenching so tightly), the four-letter doozy that rhymes with "duck" comes in quite handy for me.

I am baffled by how quickly my mood can change from bright to bothered—and my three children are young. For example, when my daughter was twenty months old, she liked the idea of construction, but found much more excitement in the area of destruction: clogging toilets with toys, coloring on wall space, and getting into just about anything she could get her hands on. One morning, she found a box of super-sized tampons and carefully unwrapped every one. She then proudly displayed them all over the bathroom floor. "Mom, what are those things used for anyway?" asked my inquisitive seven-year-old son. Unwilling to horrify him with any gory details, I avoided the inquiry and yelled, "Umm, I think something is on fire in the kitchen. Got to run!"

I adore my children, but it's not possible to love every minute of mommy-hood. Recognized as the High School Female Athlete of the Year in my hometown and a collegiate tennis player for the University of Rhode Island, I was pretty good at dealing with the varying twists and turns associated with sports. But this "curve ball" of parenting is a whole new ball game.

Each stage of a child's development presents a new challenge and alleviates the pain of another that has since passed. For example, the constant alertness required for the eighteen-month-old is replaced with the defiance of a two-and-a-half-year-old. The awkwardness of a whining first grader gets traded for the annoyances of a pre-teen. No matter how we slice it, we're doomed! I've been warned, "Little kids, little problems; big kids, big problems." How comforting. I just can't wait for those teen years.

Now and then, the dumbest of circumstances can provide the biggest parental headaches, such as something as foolish as an untied shoelace when we are bolting to the bus stop in the morning. Why is it, though, at school I can see dozens of untied shoelaces and not even be fazed? Matter of fact, I'll freely and willingly volunteer to help each student tie and re-tie, if need be. Yet, with my own child, it can spark feelings similar to that of fifty tiny spiders inching their way up and down my spine.

I have come to realize that it's not the "it" that bugs me, but more importantly, the recurring pattern presented by my own child. It's not the shoelace, at all, but rather the lack of effort made to complete the task in a timely fashion. It's behavioral! Not to mention, it's the same routine everyday, and yet each time it's as though we're starting from square one. I have experienced a bit and I have a lot to learn. But, in today's society, people are constantly being fed strategies on how to deal with their children's actions. Things such as, "I notice you're sharing nicely, Johnny;" "I like how you are playing with those toys, Lucy;" or "What should you be doing, Fred?" "I see you are frustrated, Tina;" "Your behavior is making me sad, Teddy" . . . blah, blah, blah. These observations and expressions can be effective at times, but geez Louise, it sounds rehearsed and phony. Who talks that way?

My friend Jill had recently given birth to her second child. Her newborn suffered from acid reflux, and Jill suffered from the inconsolable cries coming from her baby. She remarked that

with baby number one, she was so calm and forgiving; she never imagined using a harsh word or thinking an ill thought. Now add a second child, and welcome, mental f-bomb!

No doubt, I try to point out the positives that I notice in my own children. Yet, when my kids present undesirable behaviors and choose not to make the best choices, often they meet my parental alter ego, the "Dragon Lady." This is not the fun, spirited, smiley-faced woman that they are used to. This person is firm and downright fierce. If one of my children has provoked Dragon Lady to appear, watch out! She has been known to exhale fire from her nostrils and speak in a tone that could rattle a house.

My children are not perfect; I don't want them to be. They will make their share of mistakes. However, while I watch them perform the Malachi Crunch on each other, I'm not ashamed to say that I can become furious. My children need to recognize when I am unhappy. If all I use is "soft talk" and negotiations, I am left with chaos. Dragon Lady has appeared several times. My children don't like when she comes, but boy, how effective she can be. Trying to stay calm is important, but I shouldn't have to bargain with my children for good behavior.

I think back to when my mother used to blow her top. It didn't happen often, but many moons ago, my sister Beth and I had flipped the switch and we witnessed a different Mommy in action. Our sibling bickering had tipped her scale of patience. For a woman who typically moved slowly, her sudden speed was impressive. Instantly, the chase was on. Her turtle-like pace was replaced with the speed and agility of a tiger on the hunt. I'm not sure what she had planned for us once we were caught, but the expression on her face was not reassuring. The pursuit began in the living room, scampered through the dining room, past the kitchen, and ended in the den. We ran many laps around and around our L-shaped couch, nervously giggling as my mother looked ready to blow. Somehow we knew (or else we hoped), as mad as the look on her face was, she couldn't possibly hurt us—could she? We circled halfway in one direction, and then quickly headed in the other. Finally, she jumped over the couch and grabbed hold of both of us. Rats, we were caught. I was laughing so hard I lost all strength and was unable to escape. My mother had won and with that, we laughed, hugged, and apologized. During that episode, we felt her fury and witnessed the fire in her eyes. However, as much as she looked like a tiger on the outside, she was a gentle lamb on the inside, capable of only spreading love and sensitivity, never hurt or pain.

Last summer, as my kids ran aimlessly around my friend Kate's yard, I couldn't help but think how adorable they all were. My youngest yelled, "Look Mom, I'm a chickmunk!" as she spun in place over and over again. Unfortunately, it was time for the fun to end. I announced the five-minute warning and then yelled, "Time to leave!" How quickly the scene changed. Finley immediately ran in the opposite direction, Nolan began to sulk, and Jane started crying hysterically—actually, howling would be a better way to describe the sounds coming from her three-year-old mouth. I made a mad dash for my youngest, while Nolan reluctantly made his way to the car. But Jane's performance was the real treat. Honestly, I needed the skills of a champion jujitsu wrestler in order to buckle her wiggly ass into that car seat. With every buckle, she unbuckled. Not to mention it was 190 degrees on that humid summer day. I felt as though my head was going to burst off my shoulders. I wanted desperately to unleash the laughter, but realistically the list of offensive words flashing across my thoughts was much more comical.

I am certain that, just as I was sensing an inner upset with my children, my own mother must have felt that same sensation with my sisters and me. One can only imagine the mental f-bombs dancing through her days. As a young child, we never heard the expletives out loud, but now as I've grown, it is reasonable enough to assume that they were most definitely there, carefully concealed beneath the surface, providing her the same release from the regular pokes at her parental patience as I experience, some thirty years later, with mine.

4.
Cherish Your Mother

All that I am, or hope to be, I owe to my angel mother.
—Abraham Lincoln

I once chatted with a woman in her sixties who had recently lost her mother. After speaking with her at length about the sadness of loss, and what a terrible void she now had, she ended the conversation with three simple words: "Cherish your mother." Never did that statement ring so clearly until I became a mother myself, because, quite frankly, no one loves us like our mother.

Mary Jane Millard was born in 1942. I never had the pleasure of meeting my maternal grandparents, and have seen them only in black and white images, but I am forever indebted to them. So much of my mother's spirit lives in my soul. Her deep voice and dramatic flair create a true presence. She's almost always dressed in some shade of black and is rarely seen without a large brimmed hat on her head (worn properly at eyebrow level), and her love for costume jewelry, especially amethyst and silver rings (one on every finger), does not go unnoticed. Undeniably, she is quite eccentric.

She is quick-witted with a keen intuition. She has been, and will always be, my biggest fan. She has three daughters whom she has loved equally, yet differently. She can read each of us like pages in a book and knows our every intricate emotion. Her political beliefs are intense. I don't always agree, and at times, it may seem to her that I am not even listening, but I am. Thankfully, she challenges me to think and be aware of the many issues facing our world. She has always believed in the power of The Force—a true Star Wars fan! Acting as the Obi-Wan in my world, she is the wise sage forever reminding me and my sisters to believe in ourselves. *Be brave. Be strong. Don't settle. Don't try to people-please. Be true to yourself.* Her positive reinforcement and continued encouragement throughout our life has been paramount. We can't help but love the "lady in the hat."

My mother lost both of her parents by the age of twenty-three. Her mother died in a house fire and her father died eight months later from cancer. She was just a kid herself when her lifeline of support vanished. No parents to pick her up and pat her on the back to tell her it's going to be okay. She understands what it feels like to be let down. She lived my biggest fear as a child: the loss of a parent. Like the classic Disney tale, nobody ever expects to be in Bambi's shoes when his father delivered the dreadful message, "Your mother can't be with you anymore." She felt that heartbreak and experienced that true pain. However, she has lived through the darkness, battled her own personal issues, and somehow prevailed. She has demonstrated the reality that people can get through the challenging phases of life, and as a substance-abuse counselor, she pulls many people out of the emotional wreckage they have gotten themselves into and somehow helps them find hope.

I can still hear my mother's voice when she called the hospital the morning after Nolan was born. MJ (as we call her) had already come to see our new addition, but she had telephoned first thing the next morning to see how we all were feeling. The 24/7 hotline to her heart was in full effect, as usual. She began by saying, "You're doing so well. He's so lucky to have you." I couldn't respond because my chin had gone into complete cramp mode, and if I had started to form sentences, I would have become a blubbering buffoon. It was after the birth of my first child that motherhood became more understandable. As I held his toasty-warm body in my arms, I was able to appreciate my own mother's immediate and unconditional love for her three girls. As a teacher, I fully appreciate the importance of a good substitute, but quite frankly, there is absolutely *no* substitute for a good mother!

Growing up, my mother had a knack for entertaining her three kids. Whether it was dressing up in funny costumes at our birthday parties or conducting mock séances in order to communicate with good spirits, she was always quite the character. Without a doubt, though, one of my fondest memories of MJ occurred at my college graduation. On that day, the graduates were to walk around the perimeter of the quadrangle before taking our seats for the commencement address. When I first began to stroll, I immediately spotted my family. They were all clapping and cheering as we walked by. I could hear my mother yelling frantically, "There's Christine! David, quick, get the camera!" Then about a hundred yards later, I spotted my mother . . . again. She had pushed right through the crowd in

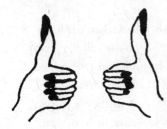

order to give me another giant thumbs up. I say "giant" because MJ has always been one to wear her thumbnails quite long. At that point, my tears immediately began as we continued our stroll. Then two hundred yards later, there she was once more, mixed into the sea of families, another two thumbs up. Well, that began the water works. It felt like my heart was being squeezed. The thought of her bustling through the packed crowd to make that connection was the best. It was the moment!

Yet with all of the goodness, I also recognize that our relationship does not always play out like a Hallmark greeting card. Her ability to be cynical can be aggravating at times, especially to me, the one who has always seen the glass half-full. We certainly have our differences, but I'm learning to accept them. Mothers accept their children's faults and annoying behaviors—do we do the same for them?

Once, after a disagreement between my mother and me, she sent me a card. On the front was a picture of a wolf peering out from behind a pine tree. The words inside read, "I've been watching." That sort of captures the essence of being a mother. Watching, waiting, and always there to protect . . . if needed. My mother still wants to protect my sisters and me and shield us from any sadness, hurt, or letdown that we may experience on this journey.

A friend of mine e-mailed me a message describing the sermon she had heard at church regarding a mother's love. The priest explained the notion that we first learn the power of love from our mother. He mentioned that the bond between mother and child may just be the closest thing to the power of love that whole religions are based on.

A mother's overall influence on her children is huge. My entire life, I have rested comfortably in the glow of my mother's love—a complete bonus for my emotional safety and security. I couldn't quite grasp that concept as a youngster, but as I have aged, I feel the intensity in my heart for my own three children and recognize that a mother's protection is instinctive. Just observe a mother bird trying to safeguard her nest—don't go there!

When a mother asks her child, "How are you doing?" she honestly cares about the response, wholeheartedly and completely in tune. I realize the undeniable fact that my own mother provides a genuine concern for me that no one else can ever possess: no-strings-attached, unconditional love. But a mother's love is not always easy. Kids can choose to demonstrate such un-lovable behaviors, yet a mother's love endures.

One afternoon spent hanging at a local playground with my kids, I utilized my gift to gab with a woman who sat breast-feeding her six-week-old infant. While the mother sat nursing, her other two children began to annoy one another on the jungle gym. She willingly revealed to me that her oldest son had ADHD (Attention Deficit/Hyperactivity Disorder) and admitted that it was becoming more difficult to remain patient, yet she thought she really needed to be doing more. Fed up with his sibling, the boy with the jack-o-lantern teeth began to pester his mother—still with the baby at her breast—to join him for a game of chase. "Come on, Mommy, chase me, already!" The boy became frustrated when his mother refused. He continued

to grunt and groan for the next few minutes and then screamed, "You are so stupid. I wish Daddy was here!" Ah, the thankless job of motherhood.

As mothers, we are often fighting a daily battle, physically and emotionally. Most children seem to present such an unfair, and oftentimes, bizarre rapport with their parents: "Because I love you and feel safe in your care, I will now torture you." How sweet. We, no doubt, possess the uncanny ability to withstand our child's occasional verbal assaults and unending blows aimed right at our hearts, but, like the ultimate boxer, mothers can't be knocked down.

To the mothers of the world, I grant each a simple head nod—no answers, no magic solutions, just the acknowledgment that we are doing a very difficult job and we are doing it quite well. My hope is to remind women that they are the most valued ingredient for their families' overall existence and happiness. There may be no exchange of golden doubloons, but that doesn't take away from the reality that motherhood is a huge responsibility. When I think of my own mother, I realize how often she provided the endless cuddles and arm tickles, and wiped away my tears with smiles and kisses. She can appreciate, first hand, what complete exhaustion feels like and knows all about the late-night march. She did it. She experienced the craziness associated with raising children. For her patience, kindness, and genuine gift of concern, I will forever remember to cherish my mother.

5.
Just Ducky

Some days, I'm just barely getting by. The water line is rising right up to my nostrils. I often wonder how it's possible to wake up happy and then suddenly feel like I'm experiencing symptoms of a mild heart attack while my eyeballs are being poked with toothpicks.

A few years ago, someone had made reference to the expression "just ducky." I always assumed the meaning to imply that everything's just fine; no problems; hunky-dory. When we observe a duck on a pond, we notice the calm. The duck looks relaxed as if nothing could possibly bother it. The sunshine is beaming down and the duck is truly at peace. But, if we took a look at what's going on under the water, we would observe a much different scene. Those duck's feet are continuously kicking at top speed. Constant movement. That's how I feel on most days. So calm and cool on the outside, but often feeling that continuous motion under the surface. I have to keep moving in order to stay afloat. I keep treading . . . kick, kick, kicking. Just like a duck.

As a point in fact, I recall the days of toilet training Nolan, first-class fun for the eight-month pregnant mother! My little bundle of love would sit patiently on that potty seat for ten to fifteen minute intervals. I would ask, "Are you sure you don't have to go?" Unconvincingly, he would reply, "Nope, I don't have to go, Mommy." He would then pull up his pants and engage himself in another activity. The routine was annoyingly predictable because within five minutes (which seemed more like thirty seconds), he would have an accident. Pants soaked, lots of tears, paper towels, cleaning spray, another load of laundry, and then try again. For two full weeks, this scene carried out throughout the day.

After four days of staying close to home, in order to practice consistently, we finally decided to venture to my parent's house for a cookout. Completely drained by the whole process, it was only a matter of time before my exposed nerves were going to get scratched. My husband was lucky enough to not really be involved in the potty training stage. He was, however, very *unlucky* to catch my wrath as we drove to the backyard BBQ. His initial response of, "It's not rocket science . . . what's the big deal?" sent violent spasms straight to my cerebellum. Oh, what a very silly man. How could he step so blindly into that minefield and be such a blockhead? Forget Dragon Lady. I became Dragon Bitch. Fortunately for him, we were within miles of my parent's home so the tongue-lashing was an abbreviated version of what could have been a long-winded rant.

I often lean toward the lighter side of an issue; I love to laugh. But, I must say, some days aren't comical. It was not funny the day I exited the beach with my three little children, and Finley, fit to be tied because we were leaving, purposely rolled her wet body in the sand. The feeling of that sand-covered body scraping against my armpits did not evoke a gleeful cackle. Nor did I giggle when I raced into a grocery store at six o'clock in the morning to buy last minute supplies needed for my son's school project that was due by 8:40 a.m.

Recently, while showering, the water had switched from delightfully warm to freezing cold. While I stood frozen, covered in soap suds, clenched fisted, waiting and cursing for the warmth of the water to return, I suddenly thought about the similarity between that scenario and the feelings we mothers have in our daily lives. We never jump out. We endure the painful moments, clench-fisted, hoping for the good times to come back. Just as we understand that the pleasant feel of warm water will, in time, return as well.

I believe that parenting is a risk worth taking, but at times I do feel like an "emotional meteorologist." Reporting on the children, I could predict sunshine with a warm breeze. Seconds later, that forecast could switch to intense thunderstorms with whipping winds . . . Close all windows! Then back to sunny skies, to pouring rain, or even throw in the old blizzard-like conditions . . . buried knee deep . . . I just don't know with my kids. While I ride out the individual storms and wait for the skies to clear, the anticipation of what's to come is tiring. Not that I expect the worst; I'm not being pessimistic, but rather realistic.

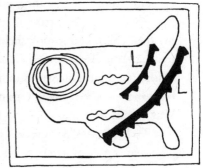

At any age, children have the ability to craze and then amaze within seconds. One morning, my son struggled (once more) to tie his shoelaces. He had been straining to get those laces tied for about five minutes. While I raced to pack the lunch bag, grab the backpack, and buckle my daughters in their car seats, he still sat on the floor with only one shoe secured. In order to get to the bus stop on time, we needed to hurry, so I became frustrated with his inability to quickly get the job done.

Later that day, while teaching a first-grade class how to jump rope, a student became frustrated with her inability to master the skill. She seemed sad so I assured her that it was a very difficult challenge and reminded her not to worry; in order to improve, it would just take some practice. At the end of the class, I pointed out that most first graders struggle with jumping rope and that I, in fact, had the same problem when I was younger. While I was giving my pep talk, I was unexpectedly interrupted by a wide-eyed six-year-old gal. She stood right up in front of the class and declared, "Every flower blooms on its own, just like every child learns when they are ready—so don't worry!" I was stunned. I couldn't have said it better myself.

How did that wise first grader know that I had needed that exact cue on that particular day? Here I was, agitated with my own child, and it took such a young messenger to remind me that I needed to relax. Kids will get it. It just takes time. Without a doubt, life works in mysterious ways. As if someone high above reaches down, taps us on the shoulder, and shouts, "Pay attention!"

We have all had moments of failure. They're not fun, but let's give ourselves a break. The daily aggravations associated with life, home, and parenting are here. We each have our own level of tolerance and capability to handle stress. We're all different. Most of the time, we are just looking for validation, and nothing feels better than when we get it. As friends, we should be there with open arms. No judging allowed. Women ought to be able to express themselves. We should be bold enough to admit when things are difficult and not feel guilty about the revelation. If a friend is experiencing difficulty, instead of barbecuing them on the grill with opinions, reach out a helping hand and just listen. We just want to be heard. We're usually not looking for an excerpt from the Parents Code of Proper Conduct. However, if the hairy eyeball of judgment looks down on us, the guilt settles in and that's unfair.

Accept that most people are kick, kick, kicking right along with us while we struggle to teach some valued virtues to our children. We all aspire to gently paddle through the day, coasting at a casual clip, but with little tots at our side, that's not always an option. Therefore, the next time your head starts spinning like a Ferris wheel, and some fool asks, "Hey, how's it going?" quickly respond, "Oh, just ducky!"

6.
Value Your Friendships

Through sunshine and shade. I heard that expression used one time and I just love it. For me, it sums up the essence of a valued friendship. Good friends remind us how lucky we are. They're true champions of the cause; the people who encourage our strengths and accept our weaknesses. They can enter our lives at the moment of literal breakdown and with just the simple sound of their voice assure us that everything is going to be okay.

My girlfriends who have shared their love and their lives are priceless beyond compare. The ones that rocked the high school dance floor to Salt-N-Pepa's "Push It" and were privy to notice my every ridiculous moment have always occupied a special place in my heart. From my days spent lip-synching "99 Red Balloons" combined with my air-popping moves to "Mr. Roboto," it's a wonder they are still willing to be my friend.

One of the funniest aspects of teen-hood was getting "set up" for a date with another classmate. As awkward as it was, quite frankly, there was no one better at it than my best bud, Sarah. I'm talking about the girl who wore the other half of my Miz-Pah necklace—the BFF that eagerly dialed up the next cute boy on her rotary style phone to see if he was interested in playing a friendly game of spin the bottle with me. *Ring, ring, ring.* "Hello, Dave? Hey, this is Sarah. What's up? Do you have a girlfriend? You don't. Well, Chris thinks you're cute. Oh, you're not sure? Well, why don't you give her a call? She's got a real good personality." Hey, how could he resist? My hair drenched in Aqua Net, puka shell necklace, white Pony sneakers, fresh Levi's cords, and a training bra . . . Come on, I was hot!

Well, twenty-five years later, she is still the girl to make the call and chat. Anytime, any place. She has listened, shared, laughed, cried, confided, and her immediacy for availability has never been taken for granted. Our topics of conversations have most definitely transformed over the years. We've traded in our acid-washed jeans and our matching canvas fanny packs for a more fashionable wardrobe with stylish handbags and accessories. The Clash's "Rock the Casbah" has been replaced with The Wiggles' "Hot Potato, Hot Potato." Forget about that party at her freshman dorm, now we're headed to her son's birthday party at Monster Mini Golf. We used to swap many stories about *90210* and *Melrose Place*, but somehow sippy cups, Pampers, and Enfamil have become interesting topics of conversation.

Back in junior high school, a particular group of girls used to verbally torture my friend Sarah and me. One afternoon, as our school bus slowly cruised along, the antagonist and her pals were up to their usual tricks. They were complaining that my friend and I were sitting in their seats. During the ride home, I stood up in order to pass my backpack to Sarah. At that moment, the leader of the pack announced, "Yo, Chris, Audrey don't want your fat ass in her face!" That was it—my personal crusade for justice had begun. I had been very patient and forgiving, but it was now finally time to take on the challenge of bringing down the brute and her awful regime. I'm not sure of the exact details after we exchanged knuckle sandwiches, but I can still feel the pain of hair being yanked from my scalp. Ouch!

I had to show some guts to confront the neighborhood nemesis, but once I did, there were never any more problems. I guess we can all benefit from a little hair pulling. Not that we want to go looking for a *Jerry Springer* slugfest, but if someone in our life is causing distress to someone we care about, it's important to address the issue. ·

The friends who have entered my life have all stamped their message somewhere within, reminding me exactly where I have been, like a passport. When I think of those stamps on

a page, I recall the fabulously funny adventures I've been on and realize that each person has provided me with something. It's often the little things: a card in my mailbox, a chat over coffee, or the simple sound of my cell phone ringing. Seeing the name of one of my friends on the caller ID screen signifies that someone wants to talk or maybe just say hello. To be thought of is nice . . . it makes me smile.

I was a social butterfly in college. I never imagined myself to be the sorority girl type, but after some peer pressure from friends, I agreed to sign up for Fall Rush (a period of three weeks where you get a sneak peek at each house on campus) and give it a try. I had all of the typical stereotypes of sorority girls and Greek life in my head—a herd of obnoxious coeds rah-rah-rahing all around campus—but, I must admit, I was pleasantly surprised and most definitely proved wrong. Not only did I enjoy it, I eventually became the president of our chapter. Note to self: don't feed into stereotypes.

Sharing a house with sixty girls is interesting, to say the least; constant stories, occasional drama, and limitless late-night pizza. During my college days, I gained twenty pounds of pure blubber—enough to make any emperor penguin sick with envy. I guess I had the concept of six-pack abs confused because double-fisting a half dozen Budweisers can surely make a belly bulge. Anyhow, was everyone in the sorority my best buddy? No. However, recognizing and dealing with the varying morals, values, and differing attitudes of each individual was a learning process in itself. Some people remained at the acquaintance level, while others worked their way deeper into my soul. Believe it or not, as hectic as that living arrangement was, I actually felt disoriented when a few friends and I moved to a house off campus for our final semester. It was quiet . . . too quiet.

Take a moment to reflect on all of the travels we have had. Focus on the important details along the way. It is through these people and experiences that we recognize how good life can be. These memories all have a voice, so let them be heard. It's obviously more difficult in our busy lives as parents to keep those friendships active, or to get new stamps in the imaginative passport. I see it already. During the early years of marriage there were constant get-togethers and continuous options for social enjoyment. Now, the infrequency of the gatherings and the inconsistency of visits from out of town friends are apparent. It's sad. But, no matter how busy I get, if the friendship is valued, I at least make an effort. Even if it's once a month, I set a date on the calendar and follow through. The rewards in the end are worth it.

Not too long ago, I had made plans with my friend Kate to go out to dinner. That afternoon, I was completely exhausted from all of the day's events. I could barely muster up the strength to prepare the gourmet Kraft mac and cheese for my family. It would have been easy to cancel. I could have gotten the kids through dinner and baths and pulled the covers over my head and gone right to bed. But I didn't. Instead, I cracked open a Diet Coke, got dressed, and dragged myself out the door. Thank God! Had I cancelled, I would have missed out on a delicious margarita, yummy appetizers, and great conversation with a close friend. Even when we're drained, emotionally and physically, we must put down the macramé needles (that wall hanging of Elvis can be worked on later) and seek out the fun in others.

If we have friends who spread the joy, it's worth recognizing. Let them know exactly how important they are to our overall happiness. The beauty of real friends is their ability to dig us out of the ditch, dust us off, and hopefully find a bit of laughter among the sorrows. If we are fortunate enough to have friends like this, we need to go find them, give them a giant hug, and tell them just how much we love them. Good friendships should be treasured because those smiles they place on our heart can be some of the brightest ones of all.

7.
As Long as You Have Your Health . . .

Being a mother of young children, I have mastered the ability to shower within a sixty-second time period. I liken my quickness to shampoo, condition, shave, and soap to the speed necessary of a NASCAR pit-crew member. When Nolan was a newborn, I would place him in his bouncy seat on the bathroom floor and begin my race. God forbid I be out of sight for three minutes. The cries usually started as soon as I disappeared behind the shower curtain. One morning, while I repeatedly checked to see if he was all right, the foaming shampoo oozed into my eyeballs. The stinging sensation of burning retinas was rather unpleasant. Nolan, of course, was fine. However, I cannot say the same for my ridiculously red eyes. They remained semi-blinded for a good portion of the morning. Not to mention, my eyeballs were already a pretty shade of scarlet due to the physiological effects associated with exhaustion and the occasional crying of a new mother. Now they were completely messed-up. I sure did have a way of looking rather swell during those early phases of motherhood. At least, with the clouded vision, I could avoid the true reflection of myself in the bathroom mirror.

Considering that years had passed and two more children arrived, I assumed it was finally safe to shower without major concern. Rethink, Chris! At twenty months, my youngest seemed less inquisitive about all of the things located in our upstairs bathroom. I thought she had seen everything and was now a bit bored with what was available at eye-hand level. I was mistaken. While I was showering, Nolan was on the computer, Jane was watching a TV show, and Finley was in the bathroom with me . . . or at least I thought she was. The warmth of the water felt great. I was enjoying every second. Suddenly, Jane shouted, "Mommy, Finley has black stuff all over her mouth!" Obviously soaked, I ran to capture the escapee. Her mouth was covered in black mascara—lips, teeth, and tongue. She had found it in my pocketbook and used it like ChapStick—big black smile and all. Bravo to Jane! Had she not sent out the alarm call, Finley could have found an even more destructive way to use it. Luckily, a quick swipe with a diaper wipe and the mascara was gone—a mild incident that could have been much worse.

Despite all of the foolishness, I have come to realize that nothing is really that terrible, as long as we have our health. That sure is hard to remember in the middle of my child's tantrum or an argument between siblings over who gets to sit where for the car ride to New Hampshire. It was a tough concept to swallow, the day Nolan threw a rock at the window and *surprise, surprise* it broke. When my daughter refused to get a much-needed hair cut and jerked  wildly in my arms for twenty minutes (as if vampire blood was pumping through her veins) while the hairdresser struggled to get it done, I certainly wasn't reflecting on my clean bill of health. On the other hand, after I've thrown the mental f-bomb in my brain and allowed some time to pass, I can begin to appreciate that I'm not at the local children's hospital dealing with some horrific news given to me by a physician.

When Nolan was twenty months old, he was required to have a CT scan because his pediatrician believed his head circumference was measuring consistently off the charts. As a precautionary step, she believed it was best if we had it done. Watching my child lie still in an anesthetically induced sleep was enough to remind me that, as long as my family was healthy, nothing else really matters. Thank goodness, the test results were completely normal; nonetheless, the experience itself was disturbing.

Three years ago, my friend Jackie's mother was diagnosed with Alzheimer's disease. She has likened the situation to that of mothering a young child and has explained the somewhat comical, yet often sad, accounts of her mother's "two hours, twenty questions" routine: a consistent repeated cycle of the exact same set of questions. "Now, which one are you? What's your son's name? Whose house is this? . . ." Since the decline, Jackie and her sisters have been sharing the role of caregiver. They are giving their mother back the gift of love, humility, and kindness that she had always given to them— mother of twelve, mind you! They are letting their mother be happy. Through the heartache and sadness associated with Alzheimer's, her family has been trying to seek the laughter and notice a lighter side of the disease; extremely hard to do, but what an important gift for their mother.

Recently, she asked her mom about a certain friend that was coming to visit, "What do you like most about those visits?" Her mother quietly responded, "When she leaves." Ha! Let's stay in touch with that inner honesty. Embrace that central humor that we all possess and remember life is short—laugh! Jackie's family has a legitimate reason to complain. I know that they feel completely frustrated, heart-broken, and scared. But overall, they are searching for the goodness in the often-maddening moments of parenting their parent.

When I drive by a nursing home and catch a glimpse of an elderly person peeking out of a window, I often wonder if they long for the good ol' days. Do they reflect on how easy everything was? Do they appreciate the crisp feel of fall; the silence of a winter's night; the scents of spring flowers in bloom; the happy sounds of summer? Do they focus on the simple things and erase all of the challenges? Wouldn't they just love to be young again? Maybe not, with this frenzied pace we keep.

As hard as it is to believe, we are in those good ol' days right now. How can that be? Listening to my child cry relentlessly because she wants to be *five* years old rather than *two*, I am aware that every day doesn't always present itself that way. Yet, it's beneficial for me to not take life so seriously. Imagine what must go through a person's mind when they are faced with the reality that their journey on earth will soon come to an end. Will they focus on the negative? Hell no! They will paint the prettiest picture of all and their heart will ache incredibly. The love for their children and the sadness that they will no longer be involved in the journey must be depressing. Someday, when we're old and very reflective, we too will realize that none of the silly stuff really mattered. We all get caught up in the daily noise, but, at the end of the day, if we have our health, it's only fair to realize that we are the lucky ones.

If our heart is unhappy, think of all the people who love us. Reflect on the lives we've affected in positive ways and appreciate the impressive job we have done in our own life. Delight in the pleasure we bring to others. Examine what we've given to our children. Do they even know who we are, other than the woman in constant motion? Will they inherit our zest for life? Are they influenced by the excitement, the independence, and the enthusiasm of us, or will the undesirable character traits of the miserable Mr. Krabs from *SpongeBob Squarepants* take hold of who we actually are? We are going to be disappointed, frustrated, and generally pissed off, but someday we are going to be gone. So, how do we want to be remembered?

I appreciate when life falls neatly into place. But, when life throws the likely disturbances, it's important for me to remember the notion that I *will* get through this, as long as I have my health.

8.
Life is Like a P.E. Class

I have been a physical education teacher at a public elementary school for fifteen years. While working with students in grades kindergarten through third, I have come to believe that life is like a P.E. class. As I have grown older, I realize just how important the role of physical education is at the elementary level. An effective program can set the tone of the entire building, with emphasis on fair play, kindness, apathy, overall health and wellness, problem solving strategies, cooperation, team leadership skills, responsibility, and accountability. Physical education mirrors life.

At school, my message is clear: play fair and be kind. I have this mantra posted on the wall in the gymnasium. Underneath the sign is a life-size cutout of Yoda, my favorite Star Wars jedi. Yoda symbolizes a belief for me that there is good in all of us; we just have to believe it! I'm trying to get my students to tap into that notion, just as I am with my three children at home. I want my students to try their best, accept the challenges, and work hard to achieve their goals. I have taught thousands of kids over the years. You can't imagine how many times each day the importance of honesty and cooperation play an issue. Kids have to stop tormenting each other, stick together, and have fun.

In actuality, we can all benefit from the expectations associated with tolerance. As adults, we need to play fair with our spouse, parents, siblings, friends, family members, and co-workers. Life is like a game and we can all benefit from following the rules. The majority of law abiding citizens adhere to the standards that are set by society because we realize things run smoothly when order exists. Chaos is never fun. Unless we want to spend time in the slammer, we respect the laws of the land.

Most people assume the obvious when they think about physical education: a pseudo-drill sergeant wearing a whistle around their neck, shorts hiked up to the mid-drift, socks pulled high to the knees, clipboard in hand, standing by a dangling rope demanding some poor soul to climb. Wait a minute. I was just having a flash back. My P.E. program, thankfully, stretches far beyond push-ups, sit-ups, and the occasional relay race. The idea of social interaction and conflict resolution among classmates is a constant. My students are young, yet very capable of independent behaviors. They need the opportunity to experience challenging scenarios and sharpen the skills necessary for figuring things out themselves.

All parents wish they were a fly on the wall, in order to observe what their kids are like at school. The P.E. teacher acts as that virtual fly. I observe children at play. I witness the behavioral choices and the split-second decisions kids make. If an undesirable behavior exists, it will present itself in class. I have told many friends that if they really want to learn how their child is acting socially at school, check with their early elementary P.E. teacher. The initial years are imperative because at the younger age level, play is still fun. As kids get older, peer influence, athleticism, and adolescent awkwardness become issues that may limit certain kids from truly participating.

The P.E. teacher may not know academically what's going on with a child, but certainly they will have some information to share about their basic social skills. Do they come to class ready to listen or immediately interrupt when a teacher starts to talk? Do they accept challenges or make up excuses for their limitations? Do they cheat or can they be trusted? Are they nice to their classmates or the first to tease someone that may be experiencing difficulty? Do they bend the rules or follow the exact set of instructions? Are they too aggressive or just demonstrating a positive competitive edge? Are they the one who tripped the opponent or the kid who offers a hand to help the fallen child back on his feet? Can they shake off the fall or is the tolerance for pain limited? Who will be the quitter and who doesn't even know what that word means? Not to mention the complainer, whiner, and the blamer. Obviously, the questions are endless, but these are just a few observations I may witness in a fifteen-minute tag game.

In life, we're all going to struggle with something. Gymnastics and figure skating were a nightmare for me. But hey, who cares? When was the last time I needed to cartwheel across a balance beam or demonstrate the triple salchow? I had a student years ago who immediately quit when something became difficult or didn't go his way. He possessed the classic glass-half-empty mentality and his belief that it was always everyone else's fault wasn't winning rave reviews from his teammates. One day, during a game of mat ball (played like kick ball but with varying rules that allow for tons of action), he finally expressed, "Games are much more fun when everyone uses teamwork and tries hard." Bingo! My message had finally sunk in, slowly but surely.

The life lessons learned in a simple activity or game carry over so nicely into our everyday world. I tell my students in class that one of the best gifts we can give to someone is our trust. It costs nothing and yet it's worth more than gold. Think of our friendships. What a comforting feeling to know we have confidence in a friendship, and what an unsettling feeling of insecurity if we don't.

When I was in sixth grade, an awkward scene played out at my birthday party. Two friends had bought me Def Leppard cassettes. Oh yeah, eighties rock: men with hair-sprayed mullets, marvelous make-up, black leather platform boots, and spandex. Wicked awesome! Laura had given me an older Def Leppard cassette, and Natalie had bought the new release. After the presents were opened, one particular guest was making fun of Laura's present. Regrettably, she overheard the hurtful comments about her cassette not having any good songs on it. I, on the other hand, couldn't care less and was psyched to have both recordings. Yet, the fact that someone was made to feel insecure about their gift really bothered me. Not only did it spoil the party, it showed me a very undesirable side of the other so-called friend.

Parents need to be alert to the issues facing our children. Be aware of the playmates that like to stir things up (they can be dangerous), and recognize the need to devise a simple strategy to solve problems at home. Just like in a game, life has boundaries too. I am convinced that children should be held accountable and start taking responsibility for their actions. Basic guidelines can be quite simple: choices and consequences. Hey, kids, if you eat ten chocolate bars, you may have a bellyache. And, moms, if you have that fifth glass of wine, you will power-puke by sunrise. You make the choice!

When my son was in first grade, he came home from school with an abundance of pink school-distributed erasers. When I discovered them hidden in his coat pocket, I questioned, "Where did these come from?" and wondered whether or not he had stolen them. Immediately he acquired the deer-caught-in-the-headlights look and the tears in his eyes began to flow, thus answering my question. After my rant that, "We are not thieves, when you leave this house you are a representative of this family," I made it clear to him that he would have to return the erasers the next morning. His tears continued to flow, reassuring me that he, in fact, did have a conscience. The importance of the story was not the issue of the erasers, but rather that he had taken something from his teacher without asking. That's the real issue. Not the two dollars worth of rubber. During that incident, I might have looked the other way, but I couldn't. What type of kids do we want to have? What are the underlying messages being sent to our children, and are we even watching? It really wasn't a big deal, but if kids aren't held accountable at an early age, how will we reel them in when the issues become larger than a pocket full of erasers?

In my world at school, the games and activities are simply the tools by which we sharpen the skills necessary for social development, community involvement, and a love for physical activity. At the end of the school year, my speech to each class begins with, "If you have learned anything at all, I hope it was the importance of being a good person." Being a skilled athlete is great, maintaining a level of physical fitness is certainly beneficial, but being a person of good character is pivotal. My hope is that kids, as well as adults, maintain a contagious sense of happiness, value the gift of trust, and enjoy the positive effect it will have on other people.

9.
Equal Time

Oh, okay. In case one of those curious husbands has crawled into bed and is wondering where his part in the story may be, I guess I'll grant him the acknowledgment! When I had this idea to write, it was not at all an attempt to "male bash." As a matter of fact, I intend quite the opposite. You see, in the journey of life, we should be able to enjoy our experiences and share them with others. Hopefully, our mate fulfills our inner needs of love and laughter. Tensions will always arise and husbands do seem pre-set to annoy, but we need to stop verbally stoning one another when troubles brew—and boy will they ever, once kids and parenting skills are involved. For those spouses who do provide us with the comfort and support system necessary to thrive, kudos! The complimentary mate who shares the challenge is very much appreciated.

Sometimes, in the daily motion, couples don't stop to recognize one another among the clutter, never mind thank each other for the jobs they are doing. (Remembering at all times, though, that surely Mom's job is the toughest.) Do we even remember what brought us together in the first place? That initial spark may be buried deep below the history, but it is, in fact, still there. It may take a pirate's treasure map to find it, but hopefully it has endured. Keeping a little mystery in a marriage is one thing, but creating an absolute riddle is just too impossible. Who has time to figure it out? Women are usually too tired for those games.

It's easy to fall in love. The real challenge is to stay in love. It takes commitment, and some days we're just not that lovable. Add exhaustion and tension and we have a recipe for spousal distress. After a particular disagreement with my husband, my friend Danika had called to see if my kids and I would like to go to the beach. I quickly quipped, "Is it warm enough for a beach day? Because it's as cold as a winter's night over here at my house." The silence between Andy and me had not yet lifted and an emotional chill factor had settled inside our home.

During the challenging phases of child rearing, we often imagine where darling Daddy could be. He may be listening to the radio in the car while driving to work, possibly checking the scores in the newspaper from yesterday's sporting events, or talking with friends on a lunch break. Oftentimes, as the annoyances intensify, we conclude that our husband is now the direct link to our moment of unhappiness. In our mind, he has now become the exact person to blame, and for this, *he must pay!*

Mothers of young children often become clock-watchers, anticipating the moment of relief when our shift is over—for a brief stretch, anyway. If he should happen to take longer than usual, the "He'll be home soon" thought gets replaced with "Where the hell is he?" rather quickly. No one wants to be the bitter bride waiting with her friends Anger, Frustration, and Resentment until Daddy arrives. But, without the ability to disconnect, unfortunately those feelings become quite natural responses to the daily job of parenting alone.

Many of us are incredibly busy, males and females alike. Husbands can become swamped at work, leaving the wife to take care of the home front. Men should never underestimate that job . . . if they want to live a long, enjoyable life! Most dads don't get the opportunity to witness what the average day at home really looks like; those individual jolts at our tolerance to accept annoying behaviors can be tough. Not to mention, trying to keep an eye on every move our child makes (in order to limit the unavoidable bumps and bangs associated with toddlers) is exhausting. Realistically, accidents can happen right in front of watchdog eyes because it's impossible to stay alert all day, every day, each week, all year.

The majority of women become very passionate to the cause of "Mommy." Some might call it defensive. So spouses should limit the condescending remarks and keep unreasonable comments about our parenting skills to themselves. Husbands, consider yourselves warned! If a mother's job is criticized by a father who has been away from the house for the entire day, get ready for the arctic express to arrive. There is nothing more offensive and annoying than when a person who doesn't take part in the daily routine decides to critique it.

My husband and I have a pretty good parenting system working for us. He is a great father and the kids completely adore him. Not all of us have a husband to rely on. Thankfully, I have Andy. He's not perfect and he is not always there when I need him, but the times that he is, he's second to none. I admire his helpful, caring, and quite comical approach to parenting. I do believe that I chose wisely on my quest for the right mate. I had surely kissed a lot of frogs before I finally met the right one.

However, how does one slip in his parental judgment provoke immediate feelings of pure disgust and disbelief?

One day in December, I decided it would be fun to try our new digital camera and take a Christmas card picture of my three kids—what a fool I was! I was asking for trouble when I chose to photograph all three at the ages of five, two, and three months. The task required patience and the ability to remain calm. I lost that challenge. I must have snapped fifty pictures  that day, but it felt like I snapped an important blood vessel in my head as well. What a headache! Toward the end of the photo shoot, I began singing the *Teletubbies* theme song. I don't know where I came up with that for a choice, but it somehow sparked smiles on two of my kid's faces while Finley gazed off to the side. Bingo, mission accomplished. The Christmas card should have read, "The Nightmare Before Christmas."

When I relayed the whole awful experience to Andy, he couldn't appreciate what the big deal was. "What's the problem?" he asked. He honestly didn't mean to discredit my efforts, but those matter-of-fact responses are usually the ones that manage to turn something so right into something quite wrong.

When the frustrations of family life leave me discouraged, it's important that I take a break and travel—not far, but little adventures to a movie, dinner with a friend, or shopping at a favorite store. If my husband is home, occasionally I'll hightail out the door in order to change the scenery. Just dashing to

the magazine aisle at a local convenience store can do the trick. Sometimes, taking a drive to a coffee shop or a fun department store can provide just the break I need, leaving me ready, once again, to face the demands waiting back at home. These brief voyages are quite enjoyable and they enable my husband to spend time alone with the kids.

It's important for dads to be available. All aboard! Andy has the power to make our three little birds laugh out loud, so it's great to keep him involved in the entire process. It also provides him the opportunity to realize just how "easy" the job is. Most mothers want to do it all (and probably do), but it's refreshing to know that there is someone right alongside to help when it's time for momma to fly the coop. Andy and I actually adopted a calendar system to alleviate some of our own scheduling concerns. If he is golfing on Tuesday, he'll write it on the calendar. If I'm going to dinner with a friend on Wednesday, I'll pencil it in as well. We sign up, and if that day is booked, we pick another. We plan out the week and appreciate the fairness. This idea of equality makes everyone in my house happier.

Not too long ago, a few friends from college had visited. I met them over in Newport at 4:30 p.m., had a beer at the Bed and Breakfast, and we were off for a sunset cruise around the harbor. It was a pleasure to share uninterrupted conversation with pals I hadn't seen in years, without a diaper bag in sight. I think it's so important for my children to see that I have a life outside the walls of my home, especially for my daughters. Young girls need positive role models. We have to lead by example, and if we're all pining away, waiting only for the fun to occur when Daddy gets home, I think we'd be selling ourselves short. Too many women before us fought hard so that wouldn't have to be the case.

Imagine the women of the 1950s. Where was their balanced identity? Let's review a list of mind-boggling expectations from a high school Home Economics textbook titled, *How to Be a Good Wife:* "Have dinner ready. Minimize all noise. Put a ribbon in your hair. Prepare the children, take a few minutes to wash their faces and change their clothes. Speak in a low, soft, soothing voice. Don't greet him with problems and complaints. Remember that you relaxed all day waiting for his return . . ." My ass, I did! How did those women do it?

We know the fairytale of marriage; how about the reality? Some days, husbands and wives hardly even get a chance to speak. We become passing shadows among the activity, barely noticing that the other is even there. Not every scene can be played out like the lyrics of a John Denver ballad. For certain, there have been many a country crooner yodeling about heart-stopping affection, but it's hard to feel those emotions during the daily march. On any given day, some spousal relationships need to be awakened from the emotional coma they are in. It's our choice whether to resuscitate or not. Some days, we may choose the latter—it's easier to just ignore.

Even the best of bonds are tested. So if, in fact, the two of you share a love-affair life, crack two bottles of beer, two glasses of wine, or two cups of "moonshine" (whatever your celebratory beverage of choice) and toast a cheers to you. If he leaves a lot to be desired these days, grab the tequila and give it a good old-fashioned guzzle. Booze goggles always make things look brighter. The daily routine can certainly be difficult, but if we learn to effectively communicate our needs, everyone benefits from the equal playtime. It's fun! Let's not live life regretting what we should have done. Better yet, take the chance to enjoy the journey while we're still on it.

10.
The Octopus

I've come to determine that two arms are not enough when parenting young children. Recently, while exiting the pediatrician's office after my daughter Jane's yearly check-up, this belief was solidified. As the doctor examined Jane, she made reference to how well-behaved my three children were—so quiet and kind to one another. The words hadn't completely rolled off her tongue before I quickly responded with, "Give it a minute!" Sure enough, I cursed myself. Those three darlings turned from angelic cherubs to downright devils in a matter of seconds.

Once Jane's check-up was completed, she eagle eyed the play kitchen set in the corner of the examination room and felt an immediate urge to get cooking. Unfortunately, Finley had that same desire. Recognizing it was time to vacate the room, Nolan "conscientiously" grabbed the make-believe hot dog Finley was holding in order to place it back on the shelf it had originally been set upon. What seemed like a helpful gesture on his part provoked a chain of events that proved to be a toxic combination. Finley began to wail and dropped herself to the floor in hysterics. Jane refused to exit and began her crying fit as well. I actually had to physically wrestle them both through the doorway while they twisted and turned in my arms. Fumbling for the ten-dollar co-pay, with one child over my shoulder and the other tucked under my armpit, the receptionist asked, "Do you need a receipt?"

"Oh no, that won't be necessary," I responded as I made a beeline for the car—sweaty, drained, and completely annoyed!

If that experience is not enough to send a person's blood pressure off the charts, I don't know what is. I may as well have injected a batch of deep-fried chicken grease directly into my bloodstream. I probably would have registered a lower blood pressure response. How did that doctor's visit go from so good to so very bad in an instant? How did an oversized pastel piece of plastic create such a terrific mess?

While I grappled both girls out of the building (both screaming and flailing) as my son followed in tow, I could not help but think of how easy that challenge would have been had I only been made like an octopus. Each child conveniently tangled in my tentacles, as I made my way to our vehicle and drove directly to the nearest Dunkin' Donuts—medium hot coffee, cream, two Splendas.

Let's face it, mothers deserve a serious "shout out!" Single mothers, married mothers, widowed mothers, whoever you are, way to go! We are the bomb! Don't get me wrong, my children are three of the absolute sweetest, cutest, kindest, gentlest, most endearing little kids I've ever laid eyes on. Yet, within seconds, any one of them can cross over to the Dark Side and act like a real knucklehead. Don't ever be foolish enough to say, "Not my child." Pie on the face may taste good, but it certainly doesn't feel good. All kids have their own tricks; it's not fun when they choose to use them.

There are many perks to being a teacher, but one of my particular favorites is the one-year maternity leave granted to a new mother. It was the best! During that time, I had my fair share of play dates. My husband thought the get-togethers were relaxing adventures and I should feel "lucky" that I was able to participate, and fortunate not to have to go to work. Oh, what a maniac—first, for thinking it, and second, for being insane enough to verbalize it. Especially to a mother working on about four hours of interrupted sleep. Them's fightin' words.

The mere thought of women just casually chatting, as if lounging on the couch was even an option, was absurd! The idea of us sipping cold beverages under the dazzling allure of a disco ball spinning overhead while our babies played peacefully on the floor was comical. Enter reality—those so-called play dates should be renamed torture tests. No matter who was involved, there were bound to be moments when my child was not sharing, or someone got pinched, or one child may have played a little too rough. Suddenly, each fresh-faced mommy now resembled Jack Nicholson's character from *The Shining* ("Here's Johnny!") as we transformed ourselves into referees for each little mishap that occurred.

I realize the innocence; I recognize that the day will come when Jane won't want to get zipped into her pink Power Ranger costume and run freely through the house. The little bodies, tiny feet, and pint-sized outfits will get larger. The soft voice, naivety, and ability to be easily amused will mature. My capability to tickle away the sadness and entertain through my own silliness will become trickier. Those mouths with missing-teeth smiles will become crowded with braces and Nolan's phase of wearing three plastic-jeweled rings on his fingers will pass and possibly get replaced with an urge to bust a sag. The issues will change; however, it's not easy to appreciate every moment.

I look back on the days when we would transition our kids from the crib to a bed. Talk about demanding on one's nerves. My parental poise was certainly challenged when those guaranteed nap times went "bye-bye" once our tot figured out how to escape from the crib. Do we lock the door? Gate the doorway? Listening to the unending screams coming from the room or the sounds of toys being chucked against the door, I wasn't sure if that was the sound of my child or the sound of a rabid raccoon that had just stumbled upon an open trashcan. Yowzer! I particularly enjoyed the yelling: "Mommy, Mommy? Mommy! Daddy, Daddy? Mommy!" Then it switched. Suddenly the siblings' names were now being hollered, and as a last resort, the words had even shifted to, "Help!" "Can anyone hear me?" or "Ouch!" The real kicker was, "I love you." They used any tactic imaginable in order to gain an exit from that room.

Those are the moments in parenting when we wish we were quietly reading a magazine on a comfy, cozy couch with only the sounds of silence dusting the air. Reality check—the actual scene involves my child still screaming, while I tend to the unending piles of laundry, water the plants, empty the dishwasher, slam three shots of Vodka, and possibly pay some bills. Gosh, the couch was a much better thought.

As much as I am bothered by some of these daily tasks, I am aware that these are the moments in life I will miss the most. Life is sweet, with a touch of sour sprinkled along the way—not to mention sleep deprivation. The circles under my eyes are a deeper shade of brown thanks to this story.

My mother has often said that if they advertised the job of mother in the "Help Wanted" ads, few would apply . . . if any! If it was a regular occupation and our colleagues treated us the same way our children did at home, they would be fired. Between the whining, bickering, and occasional juvenile breakdowns, we would seek other employment. However, mothers don't quit and kids can't be fired. For every one of us "on the job," no one gets off easy.

Imagine the mother of three who suddenly realizes she has absolutely no diapers left in the house. She must now shuffle all three small children to the local convenience store. Bummer—nothing convenient about this trip. She will place the oldest in the stroller, the youngest in the BabyBjorn front-carrier, and then strap the middle child on her back. Now that's a woman. Groceries, errands, whatever her pleasure; this mother can conquer the world. Now, no offense, if this were a scene involving a male, no matter how desperate they got, it just wouldn't happen. They would wait until Mommy got home! We women rock!

Ten years from now, I'll look back on some of my stories and laugh out loud over the ridiculousness. Although mothers may not be routinely doted on by their children, I do believe that we are appreciated by our fellow peers who share in the responsibility of masterminding every aspect of family life. For all of the women that continue to wish for additional appendages in order to manage the madness, *Namaste*—simply interpreted, I respect you!

11.
That Face in the Mirror

In the morning, while standing there brushing our teeth, we're looking directly at that face in the mirror. It's the only part of our day when we're actually staring right into the eyes of our self, except, of course, the few checks we do throughout the day to make sure that everything is in place. Who's looking back? Do we even recognize the person or have we become somewhat of a stranger in our own skin?

I remember being on an airplane once looking down at the ground below, a few seconds after takeoff. How small it makes everyone look from way up there. How inconsequential we all seem from that height. Houses are tiny; cars are dwarfed. Everything becomes a puny version of the real thing. Yet, reverse the angle and now we start to magnify the same scene. Suddenly, the individual details start to take shape. Certain characteristics can be noticed and the complete appreciation for every person is recognized. We all have a sense of spirit within and I believe it is time we tapped into it. We need to celebrate life as much as possible because, as my sister Sharon likes to remind me, "None of us are getting out of here alive."

When staring at our reflection, we're looking at the person in charge of this life. Imagine yourself as the red star on a map—"You Are Here." Where will we go emotionally? What will we experience? Who are the players? These people are all contributing editors of our story. The friends, the neighbors, co-workers, family members—each individual person we encounter makes his/her mark. Listen to their stories.

In the early stages of parenting, there is a definite loss of our own identity. Hell, I felt like Tom Hanks in the movie *Cast Away*—stuck in a world detached from the ordinary fun. I understand how a young mother can ultimately feel a sense of loneliness. The adult world can be passing by as we stand pushing our little baby on a local playground swing. How excited we are when we're simply acknowledged and noticed—even if it is the toothless truck driver named Rusty 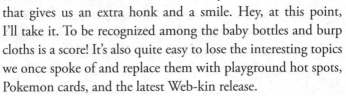 that gives us an extra honk and a smile. Hey, at this point, I'll take it. To be recognized among the baby bottles and burp cloths is a score! It's also quite easy to lose the interesting topics we once spoke of and replace them with playground hot spots, Pokemon cards, and the latest Web-kin release.

One morning, I watched my children's goldfish circle around in its bowl. The water hadn't been changed in a week and was becoming quite brownish in color. As I observed this little swimmer, I imagined our life as humans. Life is similar in many ways to that bowl: some days are murkier than others. We can sink to the bottom or try to swim towards the surface, one stroke at a time. It's usually through the "murky moments" that we learn to thrive. Just like humans, often the fish that can figure out a way to adjust to the challenges become the best survivors of all. Everyone comes with baggage (some come with a small carry-on and others come with a deluxe set), but we can all benefit from a little dysfunction-junction.

Every fresh-faced little kid starts out with a dream. Hopefully, we were encouraged to dream big. So where along the way does that change? And why? Usually, the men in our life have their ideas and they can act on those dreams and ambitions. They, no doubt, have to make adjustments as well. But I do believe that women willingly put their life, and all of its promise, on a shelf in order to parent their children—and we do it without hesitation. It's a sacrifice we gladly make, but unknowingly, it may come with a tiny level of regret.

In the musical *Les Miserables*, a dying mother sings a sad song titled, "I dreamed a dream." The character Fantine references a time gone by, when her life was happy. She lovingly expresses her affection for a man she has trusted and the life she has planned to live. However, the fantasy ends when the father of her child has abandoned her. During the last line of the song, Fantine regrettably reveals that the reality of her own unavoidable situation has destroyed the dreams she once had. We all know people (including ourselves) who allow the ins and outs of their daily life to snuff out the dreams they've dreamed.

Back in 1989, as the seventeen-year-old class president, I made a speech at my high school graduation. The message to my classmates was filled with many words of teenage wisdom. But one of the lines I remember well was the idea of not letting anyone "rain on our parade." We're all marching along in our own parade called "life." We are leading our families on this adventure. Lead well and lead wisely.

When I was about seven years old, my mother and I were on one of our shopping sprees at a local department store called Ann and Hope. For me, the outing usually included a nice browse through the aisles, a possible toy, and a definite stop at the Burger King across the street for a Whopper Jr. with cheese, small fries, and a Coke. This particular outing, I wandered through an area of coat racks and hid among the garments. Well, the joke was on me that night because I somehow lost track of where my mother went for a period of probably four minutes. I went into a complete quiet panic. I became frozen for a moment, among the polyester blouses, and then hesitantly walked out from the clothes rack. Quietly, I inched along the surrounding aisles, hoping to find her. *Where could she be?* My heart pounded as tears filled my eyes. *Where am I? Where is she?* Then from three aisles over, I heard my mother's cough, a distinct sound that ended my panic. That night I don't remember what the toy may have been or how delicious that Whopper Jr. was, but I knew something—I knew that my mother was there with me, like a blanket of safety. The simple sound of her voice assured me that I was protected.

Plenty of birthday cakes and candles later, I am now the mother. A little bit older, hopefully wiser (hey, I chucked the blue eye shadow, didn't I?), and now *I'm* supposed to have the answers. I am expected to make a "boo-boo" go away, heal a broken-hearted sob, and scare away the monsters from under my child's bed. Yet, at the same time, I long for the days when

I could lie on the couch eating Nutter Butters in my underoos while *my* mother willingly made sure that everyone was okay. We don't really have to grow up, do we?   .

We are undoubtedly providing a unique sense of security for our children while juggling a gazillion tasks at once. However, we can't lose touch with our inner self. The next time we glance at our own image in the mirror, stop! Pause for a moment and literally reflect. Stare sincerely into those eyes. Don't inspect the eyebrows. Forget about any crooked teeth. Refrain from scrutinizing the complexion. Dismiss that bump on the nose and disregard the mole on that cheek. Instead, make eye contact with beautiful, wonderful, you . . . and smile!

12.
We All Make Mistakes

Years ago, when I was in high school, I remember an incident that occurred during a softball game. My coach had lost absolute emotional control and unloaded his thoughts of my overall performance. It was the semifinals of the playoffs, bottom of the seventh inning, and we were ahead by two runs. My knees were trembling as I assumed the ready position at shortstop. It was my junior year, the bleachers were packed with cheering fans, and the pressure was on. Get three quick outs and we're done. State Championship, here we come. The pitch was thrown and the first ball was drilled directly at me. It took a weird bounce and blasted right through my legs—error number one. Now, with a runner on first base, the next batter smacked the ball straight at me again. I fielded the ball smoothly and figured I would get the easy force-out at second base. However, when I prepared to make the fifteen-foot throw to the second baseman, my arm went numb. It felt like a wet piece of overcooked spaghetti. Hence, the throw sailed over her head and wound up in the outfield—error number two. Oh boy, no outs with two runners on base. By this point, my coach was furious—hopping mad! He shouted a number of zingers my way: "That's garbage! . . . You're awful! . . . Get your head in the game!" He was fuming and I was completely humiliated. As an all-state athlete, I was usually the sure bet for an out. Quite dependable, to say the least, but at that moment I goofed up!

Thank God, we somehow managed to get the three outs and win the game. I took the tongue lashing from my coach in stride. I accepted the fault and went home. Upon arrival, my mother greeted me with her usual positive spin on the game. After not responding to her comments, she soon realized that I was sobbing. She didn't quite understand why because she had left the game before the verbal assault began. When I retold the details, she immediately wanted to make a call to the coach, but I refused. There was no way she was going to do that. Absolutely not! Sometimes we do make mistakes and it's important to recognize it and take responsibility. It certainly doesn't feel good to hear it, but had my mother made that phone call, where would that have gotten me? How would that have changed things? I still made two back-to-back errors.

We have to learn to accept who we are in this game of life and deal with the issues along the journey. We're human and no one is perfect. We are all capable of stumbling right on our faces. (Quite reminiscent of my younger years spent leaving fraternity parties. Ouch!) But somehow we do manage to bounce back up. There are so many life lessons to be learned when we walk into challenging situations. No one likes the swing-and-miss moments, but when we lose we learn to appreciate how good it feels to win. There are few things greater in life than pumping both fists in the air and saying, "Yes, I did it!" after accomplishing a difficult task. The celebratory high five is equally exhilarating.

As mothers, we're going to make our fair share of mistakes as well, especially when playing the role of household disciplinarian. With all that is expected of us physically, mentally, and socially, it is easy to see how people can crumble. It is so important to vent out the frustrations we may have and share our concerns with someone: a friend, family member, spouse, counselor, or complete stranger. Whoever it may be doesn't quite matter, as long as we can express our discontent and get through it. Yet, if we continue to bottle-up the annoyances, our emotions become frayed, like tight strings on a violin, just waiting for that moment when we're going to snap.

Nothing feels worse than true emotional tension and heartache, especially with my own kids. It's painful. Occasionally, I have said the "wrong" thing and regretted my approach in hindsight. I may not remember everything that was communicated during a particular situation, but I certainly remember the look on my child's face after an annoyance has escalated. I see the tears in their eyes. I feel the depth of their stare poke deep into my heart. The sorry look of a little blond head tilted downward is not easily forgotten. Make no bones about it, disciplining children is hard work. We're not always going to say the "appropriate" thing. Sometimes it's hard to be appropriate. But kids, as well as adults, have to learn limits. We shouldn't be afraid to say "no"—it's a powerful word.

Females often marinate in parental issues. Why is that? We women have to be allies in life. It does us no justice to compete against one another as mothers. There is no winner. We all do what works, but the key words are "what works." If our game plan doesn't seem effective, mix it up. Let's remember, no one has the *right* answers, and no one is competing for "Mother of the Year." Besides, I've already won that when I told my six-year-old, "Just stop bitching." Oops! That puts me at the top of the list. Sorry.

In recent years, I have seen many women trying to perfect something that, quite frankly, can't be perfected. Each child is different, as is each parent, each issue, and each response. What annoys one person may actually entertain another. We are all complicated individuals with quite differing needs and desires. With all of the roles and responsibilities placed on our lap, it's easy to understand that on certain days we may feel like we're losing our minds.

Case in point, I had taken my youngest to the doctor's for a sick visit. When I arrived, the nurse asked for my daughter's weight. I had no idea so she checked her chart. Not only had I missed her two-year check-up, I had missed the eighteen-month one as well. They hadn't taken a weight on her in six months . . . ahhh! I was shocked. Did I have a lobotomy? I couldn't imagine how that happened. I actually really am quite organized, or at least I was.

Of course, every baseball player dreams of cranking the ball right out of the park, preferably with two outs, the bases loaded, bottom of the ninth inning. We all secretly want to be the one cheered for by the fans and carried off the field by our teammates, but realistically, that's not usually the case. Just like that playoff game back in 1988, sometimes we goof up.

The truth is I loved that softball coach. He was fiery, enthusiastic, and full of life—a real great guy. That day, he let his emotions get to him and he lost it. That's all. Although he was painfully honest, I knew he didn't mean to hurt my feelings and that's why I accepted it. I understood that he wasn't critiquing me personally; he was upset with my performance. He knew that I was better than that and as a result, he was very disappointed.

Parents often *lose it*. The more we allow things to stew at our emotions, the bigger the verbal overflow when we finally reach our limit of patience. Most of the time, my kids don't even understand that they have upset me, until my eyes pop out of their sockets, roll a complete 360 degrees, and then resume their position back where they anatomically belong. Then they get it!

Acknowledging that we are not perfect is refreshing, and admitting that fact is quite freeing. Release, relax, and most importantly, be free!

13.
Angels Among Us

While I sit in the sunshine, a warm breeze at my back, I am reminded how beautiful this world is—the magnificent trees, varying shades of blue in the sky, and the sounds of summer bustling by. Nature has so much to offer, no doubt, but for me, it is the human contact on this journey that I appreciate most. Without human connections, I would be lost. I have encountered many interesting souls in my thirty-seven years on this planet, but how do we account for those people who enter our lives for brief moments and yet leave us with lessons that can last a lifetime?

I love believing that someone is always looking out for my family and I, and pointing us in the right direction. I'm not saying that every scenario is the best, but I do continuously try to find the good in each situation. It's probably a bit annoying to be so optimistic, but keeping my eyes and heart open for all of life's situations to unfold has gotten me where I am today. There will always be an element of risk when I'm willing to put myself out there in such a vulnerable space, but it's a risk I enjoy taking. A belief that there is an underlying reason for the chain of events, as awful as they could be, and as wonderful too, helps me cope with the craziness of my daily life.

One morning, I met an older gentleman while jogging. I was ten minutes from completing my morning run when we bumped into each other and he joined me for the last leg of the jog. I must admit, at first I thought he was a stalker, but then I found out he was a retired teacher who had just moved to the area with his wife. He described quite eloquently the belief he had about teaching. He pointed out that as a young teacher, he felt like a "chef," a true creator, bringing individuality and talent to his class. But by the end of his teaching career, he felt more like a short order cook at a chain restaurant. Everything came prepared and there was no real need for creativity or talent. Additionally, he talked about "filling the bucket" versus "sparking the flame"—just jamming information into the student instead of sparking an interest in lifelong learning. How is it that a ten-minute chat provided such an important perspective?

Whatever our spiritual beliefs may be, it can surely be fun trying to figure out the coincidences of life. How do we explain the family that fled Russia in 1980 and found their way to my neighborhood just three houses down, thus introducing me to one of my most valued and trusted comrades? Or the new person from my child's preschool who entered my life at just the right moment, reminding me exactly what good friendships are all about. Maybe it's the admiring co-worker who fills my day with kindness or the person at the grocery store who, just by looking into her eyes, assures me that my day will be all right. Each little moment provides us with something. There is a reason why these paths cross. Who sends these people in our direction hoping that we might, in fact, one day meet?

A couple of years ago, I had met a person through my son's soccer participation. At the time, Jane was only two years old and I was pregnant with Finley. My ability to watch any part of Nolan's practices or games was quite limited. I was usually found over at the playground, thirty yards away from the soccer activity. Anyway, as months passed by, I continuously bumped into this person over and over again. It became comical, as if someone up above was nudging her into my life suggesting, "She'll make a nice friend." Finally, after a year of random run-ins around town, as well as a community road race, we bumped into each other on Mother's Day and agreed to meet for a morning jog. Our connection was instant and easy. The laughter was contagious and the endless conversation flowed naturally, not to mention the ridiculous coincidences and similarities we shared. We actually attended the same high school (she graduated the year before I entered my freshman year) and her father-in-law was my mother's ob-gyn who had, believe it or not, delivered my sister Beth and I. We agreed that it was just meant to be. Ah, the fun of newfound friends!

There are certainly a few angels laughing out loud knowing that these nudges in my life, indeed, have worked. Had I never looked up, I would have missed out on many friendships that have brought so much happiness my way. I had a student whose family started a tradition called "Give me seven:" five fingers from a firm handshake, paired with two eyes looking right at the person they are greeting. We have to take the time to look at people. In this fear-based society we are living in, most people point their eyes to the ground, never once glancing up. Take the chances. Whether it's talking with a neighbor at our child's bus stop, attending a PTA meeting in order to get involved, or chatting with some parents at the next ball game, it's worth it! When we make ourselves available for goodness, we open the door to endless opportunities of joy.

About ten years ago, a woman named Michelle, who knew my husband, came into my life and left a lasting impression. Although she was someone I would only see a couple of times each year at a local tennis tournament our husbands participated in, she was the kind of person who possessed that shining bright light within. With just a few words, she invariably uplifted me. She was so kind, emotionally inviting, and fun to be around. Unfortunately, Michelle was battling cancer, a battle that she was not going to win. A few years ago, I saw her in a supermarket parking lot. She was two rows over and I was in a rush, as usual. We didn't get a chance to talk; she simply yelled across the lot, "You're beautiful," with a giant smile, and I called back, "And so are you!"

That was the last time I saw her. The cancer had won. I never had the chance to say goodbye. When I saw her at the store, I had no idea of the severity of her situation. When I heard about the decline she had taken, I so desperately wanted to send her a note. I had no luck. The address was unlisted and because I didn't know her that well, I was unsure of where to turn. Life got hectic and I just let it slide. When I found out she had passed away, I was saddened. An opportunity missed, I should have sent that card and told her exactly how beautiful she was, inside and out.

A year had passed and I was taking a yoga class in the winter. I was the laughing stock of the group—quite athletic, but with absolutely no flexibility. There was a young woman in the class who was consistently friendly, always the first to say hello and genuinely seemed interested in my well-being. Although I enjoyed taking that class, spring was approaching and my husband's tennis coaching season was about to begin; thus ending the opportunity for Saturday morning yoga.

Months later, I bumped into that friendly faced girl at the supermarket. She was standing with someone that I had given tennis lessons to several years ago. We got talking and somehow my husband's name came up. Both of them knew him from his years as a teacher and coach in our town. In fact, the young woman from yoga mentioned that her parents knew my husband. I asked, "What's your last name?" As soon as she answered, I realized she was Michelle's daughter. This wonderful person, so friendly and bright, was a beautiful reflection of her mom. I told her the story of my missed opportunity and shared my sincere affection for her incredible mother.

I was grateful to have had the opportunity to talk about how much her mom had meant to me. I should have sent that card, but I do believe that Michelle already knew exactly how I felt. The admiration I had for her was written all over my face each time we crossed paths.

Such brief flashes, but in the end it's important to make eye contact and involve ourselves with the world around us. Who knows, we may experience those "friend-at-first-sight" feelings and share the smiles! However, if we're too busy focusing our eyes on the cracks in the sidewalk, we can surely miss out on the endless possibilities. Give me seven!

14.
Appreciate What You Have

We are most definitely living in a time of endless opportunity for fun. Our financial status has enabled my children to enjoy many of the programs and activities offered in our community. Economically, it doesn't burden us to take the kids to see *Sesame Street Live* or *Disney on Ice*, but at what point will my children realize this is special? Between visits to children's museums, aquariums, local zoos, and a few opportunities to see live-action theatre (*Lion King* and *Cats*), it's hard for my kids to understand that those experiences are a treat.

All of these enrichment opportunities are certainly well received by my children, but definitely a far cry from my childhood experiences of playing with Matchbox Cars and firecrackers in the backyard. With all this stuff we have, I'm fearful that my children may become ungrateful or overindulged. Have children in today's society learned that they absolutely deserve whatever their little hearts desire?

When I was a kid, there were no Broadway shows attended or extravagant vacations taken. We skied a few times a year. We made the annual family trip to New Hampshire in the summertime, stopping at Story Land and Santa's Village—the northeast parent's rite of passage—and we made one venture to Disney World when I was eleven years old. These days, kids make several visits to Disney by the time they've celebrated their sixth birthday.

My parents always dealt in cash—no ATM and very rare uses of their credit card. We lived within our means. If we couldn't afford it, we didn't have it. We grew up in a modest ranch house, which my parents still live in today. We were all expected to get a job and realize the value of earning a buck.

My mother and father drove affordable cars and kept them until it became an actual safety hazard to have them on the road. In fact, the metal floor panel of our station wagon (where the driver's foot rests) was worn through so badly you could actually see the roadway under the automotive carpet square. "Just buy another piece of carpet, no one will ever know the difference," was my father's response to the possible danger.

Nowadays, people possess season passes to just about every venue imaginable and the marketing geared towards children has become tremendous. Air travel is much more affordable, video games considerably better, and there are round-the-clock cartoon networks, loads of toys, and limitless extracurricular activities. Recently at school, I actually overheard two young third graders discussing iPod gigabytes and the latest edition of Guitar Hero, reminding me (once again) that times have certainly changed since the days of Donkey Kong and yellow waterproof Walkmans.

When did all of the overindulgence start? And is it setting our kids up for disaster? Nowadays, kids have spectacular birthday parties — carnival games, magic shows, traveling petting zoos, you name it. Whatever happened to cake, ice cream, and a cone-shaped hat placed on our head? And let's not forget the magnificent goody bags given at these celebrations. Some have provided more loot than the gift given to the birthday child.

Often, as I've prepared to leave one of these birthday parties, I have noticed a certain look of panic drape over many of the children's faces, each wondering where those goody bags are hiding? Soon the wonder changes to quite direct lines of questioning: "Where is my goody bag?" And on more than one occasion, I have even heard a few children question, "That's it?"

One year, I had a child arrive at a party for one of my kiddos and actually declare, "We have a problem!" I quickly responded with, "What's the matter?" She continued, "There are only two things to do at this party: eat or go in the inflatable bouncy house." *Well, isn't that interesting*, I thought. *She somehow forgot option number three: go home.* Ha! This overabundance has become the norm in their world. They are accustomed to it. They don't know any different, so how can we blame them?

Last fall, I took my three kids to the playground. At the time, they were ages six, three, and one. This was common practice, because we really do have some beautiful recreational facilities in our town and I think it's important to utilize them. That morning, it was a bit cooler in our house than it was outside. We were all dressed a tad too warm as the temperature began to rise. My friend Danika and her two children met us at 11:00 a.m. We stayed for about an hour and realized that the kids were red-faced, sweaty, and looked like they were ready to collapse. I suggested we leave, pick up some cheeseburger Monster Meals, and go back to our house to eat. At that very moment, my son began to express his immediate need for a drink. The emotional distress was intensifying with the rapid-fire repetition of "I'm thirsty." I had not packed any beverages (shame on me), but I reminded him that we were, in fact, on our way to the local burger joint, and last I checked, those Meal Deals came with an icy cold drink. This revelation did not help the situation. He continued to whine and borderline torment me for the next few minutes. I reminded him, "My fingers are not capable of dispensing cold juice, therefore, you're going to have to wait, buddy." (Mental thought translation: "Ask one more time and your ass is grass!") The comments continued. That was the moment Dragon Lady arrived. We didn't know she was invited to play, but oh my, there she was! "Get in the car," I barked at my three lovelies and then motioned to Danika, "We'll meet you at my house," as I quickly corralled my trio and buckled their butts into their car seats.

As I gassed up the engine, my lecture began. At a very high volume with my jugular vein fully engorged (I thought I actually pulled a muscle in my neck), I reviewed the facts: We did not have any drinks in the car. We were leaving in order to go get some lunch. Our friends were coming back to our house for extended hours of enjoyment. And let's not forget, young children, we started our morning playing at a beautiful playground. That, in itself, is pretty darn good. As a child, I don't remember my mother carting me around to neighborhood play areas. She was more likely to say, "Go outside and play a game of Jarts." (Remember that backyard safety hazard? I had to keep my eyes to the sky for fear that a mis-tossed metal dart might find its way into the center of my skull.)

Anyhow, my lecture continued with a story involving a former student I had in class years ago: "That girl probably rarely spent a day at the playground and never had play dates set up with friends with mutual interests." But, unlike the behavior of my child, that girl never complained. She was a kid that had every right to be mad at the world, she had legitimate reasons to bitch and moan, yet she didn't. She appreciated everything we did in class, never quit, always did what was asked, and worked well with others. She came from nothing (very poor and a product of some serious dysfunction), yet she was the richest one of all.

Somehow, the important lessons that I'm trying to teach my students at school were regrettably being missed by my own child at home: Be patient. Wait your turn. It's not just about you. Think of the group. Don't whine. Although he was only six years old, and yes, quite hot and thirsty, I saw it as selfish and an unacceptable behavior.

I understand that kids live in the here and now. I get the reality that they don't grasp all of the work involved with parenting. No doubt, a youngster's brain is not fully developed to be patient and appreciate our every effort. Heck, adults may not be so enduring either, but we hopefully learn how not to throw a fit. Kids don't have that benefit, so they just let it rip. I also comprehend that the thankful young student never had the extra opportunities for fun; therefore, each activity *was* special. She had no expectations.

However, I want my three children to understand that not everything is going to be placed on a silver platter for them. They're going to have to value what they have, hopefully notice how lucky they are, and sympathize with others who may not have the same resources or privileges. How did a simple juice box, or lack thereof, create a temporary mental disaster? Some might answer, "Next time, pack drinks." Yes, that's an obvious response, but that shouldn't be the point. If in fact we just don't have what they immediately desire, kids need to at least practice patience.

Think of the mothers that conscientiously pack the pocketbook full of snacks. It's like a darn Seven Eleven inside. Raisins, crackers, juice boxes, fruit snacks, hand sanitizer, wipes for messy fingers, etc. I was at a children's museum one day and I witnessed a mother repeatedly reach into her bag to offer a new selection to her young son. Each option she offered was met with a "NO!" and then she would kindly reach in for another. Every option was better than the previous one offered, yet this child continued to show his distaste for her choices. "No, no, no!" Finally, after five minutes of this not-so-enjoyable game, she reached for the chewy fruit snacks and the child accepted. Thank God for the chewies. I imagined what the scene would have been like when I was a kid. Number one, I would not have been at a children's museum (that was a venture taken only on a school field trip), and number two, the only option for a snack would have been a drink from the water fountain and a candy bar from the vending machine.

When I reflect on various parenting strategies, I recognize the continuous compliments and rewards given to children. Instead of just doing something, some kids will follow a checklist and receive a prize when the task is complete. If a child has participated in any type of activity or recreational sport, a trophy is received or a certificate is accepted—all wonderful practices and I'm guilty as charged . . . I do the same thing with my kids. Potty training chart with stickers—get ten stickers and reach into my prize bag. Read a Magic Tree House book; get a package of Pokemon cards. These are all very fun incentives for my kids. They absolutely love it! But I wonder if all of these rewards are setting them up for unrealistic expectations. Not everything in life deserves a sticker and not everyone is willing to offer a high five.

Admittedly, most children of today's generation are reaping the benefits of continuous amusement, but they need to consider how much work goes into effective parenting. Kids can't assume that we're going to entertain their every wish, yet if we're not setting limitations, how will they learn that lesson? Being culturally enriched is one thing, but being a spoiled brat is another. At the end of the day, the only thing our kids really need to be spoiled with is our adoring affection. Now we can all appreciate that.

15.
Touch Base with
the Teacher

Teaching is a terrifically challenging job. The education system has changed remarkably over the years and the demands placed on students for academic excellence have skyrocketed. Thanks to state boards of education, kids as young as seven years old are under a lot of pressure to maintain good grades, perform well on standardized tests, and recite eloquent oral presentations in front of their fellow peers. Geez, as an adult I still get nervous speaking at faculty meetings, never mind the fears I had as a youngster in school. Along with that, many children are expected to construct masterpiece projects, complete nightly homework assignments, express an interest in the arts, gain fluency in Chinese, and perhaps demonstrate the talent needed to play the freaking glockenspiel.

Truth be told, some teachers do not belong in the profession. In fact, a specific tyrant comes to my mind. This antagonistic teacher taught for many years at my high school. With her pencil-straight hair tied up in a bun, her black-as-ink eyes set deep into her face, and a nose as sharp as a toothpick, this woman patrolled those hallways of the English department with the ferocity of a hired henchman. Gadzooks! It's no wonder she was never nominated for "Teacher of the Year." She reminded me of a Sleestak from the T.V. show, *Land of the Lost*. And she had absolutely no tolerance for any fool posing as a badass. I look back on that day when I witnessed her unloading a verbal assault on an unsuspecting drifter. I was delivering a message to the main office when I observed her slithering up to a young man who had been cutting class. Not only was that poor soul busted for doing something wrong, he was also sporting a Jagermeister t-shirt (the most potent of alcoholic beverages) that required additional penalties for violating proper dress code. Let's just say, Madam Sleestak wasn't amused. I'm not exactly sure of the punishment inflicted upon that kid, but I think it is safe to say he wasn't found roaming in her territory of the building ever again.

Thank goodness teachers have changed. Yet, as parents, we need to be mindful that educators have the difficult task of maintaining a safe and structured environment while fulfilling each child's varying levels of skill and ability, especially at the elementary level. For example, some kids in first grade may already be reading at an upper-grade level while others in the same class may still have difficulty recognizing their letters. The balance necessary to reach the individual goals and keep everyone on task is comparable to motherhood. No teacher is perfect, just like no parent is without fault.

Realizing that our child's teacher may have a completely different philosophy than ours, it's critical to possess an ability to effectively communicate. Positive connections dismantle all of the insecurities and uncertainties relating to a particular issue or concern. Why would an educator go out of their way to create a problem that doesn't exist? It takes too much energy and valued time. We need to understand that it's not just the well-being of our child, but rather the well-being of everyone in the classroom. This may not be how we run our ship at home, but remember that their ship has a few more passengers with many more immediate expectations. Administrators, parental concerns, state mandates, and other classroom discipline issues can cloud a teacher's point of judgment. So give them a break; no bones, please.

So far, my own children have all had wonderful teachers— kind, caring, nurturing, and capable of structuring a beneficial learning environment. Each has expected respect and demanded good manners. They've recognized that all children have feelings and work best in an emotionally comfortable classroom. However, each time I have met with their teachers, I've always encouraged them to be painfully honest. I want to know exactly what my kids are like at school. It does me no good to have them candy-coat the facts. I'm a big girl and although I don't like hearing the negatives, I need to be aware that there is a possibility our little angel could be a real devil at school.

Most parents can't imagine the differing personalities and behavioral challenges that teachers have to face on a regular basis. As a teacher, I have occasionally witnessed open defiance. For example, one morning, I specifically instructed the children not to touch the hula hoops and hurdles while I was giving the introduction. Then five seconds later, while staring right at me, a student boldly made her way over to the obstacle course and started to play; the look in her smiling eyes begged the question, "What are you gonna do about it, gym teacher lady?" Quite frankly, she should have just given me the middle finger; at least it would have provided some comic shock value. Instead, I was just annoyed.

When a teacher contacts a parent with an undesirable report, it hurts. No one ever wants to hear negative news, so it makes sense that we want to avoid this for our children. However, when it comes in, we have to be gracious enough to entertain the talk. Families that accept the honest description of their child's performance are appreciated. Listen to the teacher's tale, as painful as it may be, and remember the story may be quite different than the one our child told. We certainly need to believe their tales, but often it's good practice to check the source and get the facts. A quotation that springs to mind was written in a letter sent home to parents from a school's principal: "If you promise not to believe everything your child says happens at this school, we will promise not to believe everything he says happens at home."

In recent years, I have witnessed too much blame being placed on the educators and not enough responsibility and accountability on the students. My child may get a sour apple every once in a while, but it's important to let the teacher be the teacher. If problems occur, I try to take the good with the bad and learn from the experience.

As an educator, I have learned that it's not always the curriculum concerns that matter most when trying to teach children. One afternoon, while I worked with a class outside, I noticed a boy concentrating on the flowers growing in the grass.

He carefully picked a yellow flower and then placed it in my hand. "Here, Mrs. Carr, this is for you. You deserve it." Gratefully, I took the flower. "That is beautiful. Thank you." His buddy, overhearing our discussion, joined in on the fun and they began to search for more flowers. For the next five minutes, those two boys scurried around the area searching for wild flowers—any kind or color would do. "Mrs. Carr, this one is the most beautifullest of all. Its got purple *and* yellow." "Oh, you are right," I agreed. One of the boys actually picked an entire handful of weeds that resembled baby's-breath. I said, "That looks like baby's-breath. It must be stinky." They laughed. As the bouquet grew in size, the boys became concerned. "We better get them in water. They'll never make it through the night." I reassured them that I would take care of it as soon as class was over.

It was delightful to watch those two little guys in action. My head was literally tingling while the scene of innocence played out in front of my eyes. They could not have cared less about the P.E. lesson of the day while chitchatting about flowers, but at the same time, they reminded me of a very important life lesson: kids are kids. So often we try to jam as much information as possible into these youngsters, yet we don't always have the time to appreciate the tender moments of simplicity. I wondered when the last time my head tingled while watching my own three children at play; regrettably, not that often. Usually, I'm bolting around town to the next item on the agenda and don't stop to acknowledge the beauty.

Teaching is, no doubt, a special profession. To be given the chance to work with little people and make a difference in their lives is a pleasure. But a good education takes time to unfold. Quality learning requires work and it shouldn't be rushed. I could have demanded that those two boys actively engage in the lesson; however, on that particular day they acted as the teacher for me. The most effective teachers are often the ones who manage to peek inside a student's heart and see what makes him tick. Those are the ones who really make a difference. But they can't do it alone. It takes a team effort: child, parent, and teacher. One of my favorite poems that touches upon this very concept reads as follows:

Two Sculptors

I dreamed I stood in a studio
    And watched two sculptors there,
The clay they used was a young child's mind,
    And they fashioned it with care.
One was a teacher: the tools she used
    Were books, music, and art.
One, a parent who worked with a guiding hand
    And a gentle, loving heart.
Day after day the teacher toiled
    With touch that was deft and sure,
While the parent labored by her side.
    And polished and smoothed it o'er.
And when at last their task was done,
    They were proud of what they had wrought:

For the things they had molded into the child
Could neither be sold nor bought.
And each agreed he would have failed
If he had worked alone,
For behind the teacher stood the school
And behind the parent the home.

—Anonymous

With everyone on board, our children will certainly be ready to take flight and experience the valued benefits of a quality education.

16.
The Family History

My husband and I are both blessed with the gift of sisters. A sibling of any kind, boy or girl, is a bonus. For these are the people we share the station wagon with, especially during those younger years. They know all of the family secrets (good and bad). Tapping into the memories usually reminds us of the many adventures we have all been on, both funny and sad. These people are our fierce protectors, from backyard bullies to broken hearts. They are the direct lifeline to our family history.

My sisters are both different, yet equal. We share a loving mother who has devoted her life to her three daughters. The relationship between all of us should forever be valued with great tenderness and respect. We owe that connection to ourselves, our children, and especially our parents.

Oh sure, we all have our sibling stories of battle and ache. It is, however, the job of siblings to somewhat torture each other (and our parents) during those growing years. From the "prize party" scams (after a trip to a penny candy store, my sisters would trick me into giving them each a 1/3 of my loot by enticing me to believe a party in my closet would be worth the trade) to the occasional pinch my husband received from his sister when no one was looking. And I can't forget the mini "yard sales" my sisters and I set up in the hallway: my oldest sister would occasionally suggest we have a yard sale and trade some of our toys and other stuff found in our bedroom. Beth and I would always try to find our best goodies and line them up outside of our doorway. Sharon, on the other hand, usually found the worst crap and always ended up with the best exchange in the end. Ugh!

My sisters often remind me of the annoyances I presented as the youngest in the family. I am told I was a real fireball when provoked, but as feisty as I was, I was never a teaser! I didn't like it. However, my sisters certainly enjoyed busting my beans about my imaginary friend, Johnny Monny. When I was about five or six years old, I would talk to myself out in the garage. My imagination was endless. I pretended that I fixed bicycles, skateboards, and tennis racquets. My friend Matthew lived down the street and we would spend hours playing make-believe. When he wasn't available, Johnny Monny filled in quite nicely.

How was it that those younger years always seemed to last so long? Summers seemed endless; every young kid had nothing but time on their hands. Ah, the possibilities! I can still recall the sight of the Scotty's ice cream truck slowly making its way up our street. The sound of the ringing bell created a panic among the neighborhood kids. "Mom, we need money. Hurry up. Quick, we're going to miss it. Quick!" Although

a welcomed sound to all of the youngsters, it must have been an absolute irritation to the parents of those children. When I was young, summertime meant loads of mosquito bites, scrapes, scabs, and bumps on the knees. I never could figure out how other girls kept their legs so clean and unharmed. It baffled me because I was always a mess: dirty feet and finger nails, with end-of-the-day tub water worthy of an ogre. I can remember my feet being as black as the nighttime sky. Thankfully, personal hygiene must have eventually become a concern because, surprisingly enough, later on in high school I was nominated as Homecoming Queen. Go figure.

Back when Ponch and John were patrolling the interstate, ticks were not a concern, and neither were car seats, safety belts, or lead paint. Summer was a time to put away the books and let loose. An occasional sleepover and later-than-usual bedtimes became the norm. We didn't worry about reading lists or math equations back then. My biggest concerns were whether or not I would get a chance to swim at my friend's pool, go to the beach, or make it to the July 4th fireworks display.

In those days, kids were expected to play outside— anywhere and everywhere until the streetlights came on. As a matter of fact, returning home anytime before that was a direct result of a feud that must have sparked between friends. I recall one neighbor who was never allowed to have kids come inside his house to play. It just wasn't an option. The living room in his home was referred to as "the parlor," and with both couches wrapped tightly in plastic and a dozen Hummels carefully displayed among the other chachki on a maple hutch, the room screamed "off limits!" to any person passing through to use the bathroom.

Saturday nights in the 1970s were set as date nights for my parents. My mother would ready herself in the bathroom.

I always knew it was close to departure time once the smell of Lamonte perfume entered the air. That scent mixed with a generous douse of Old Spice from my father was a sure sign that a babysitter was en route. While my sisters and I waved goodbye from the window, the maestro himself, Lawrence Welk, would be leading the gang of happy entertainers on the TV. Each gal singing on that stage was always dressed in the perfect blend of polyester, purple, and pink. I don't know which show scared me more, that or *Fantasy Island*—"the plane, boss, the plane . . ."

Often, as I have aged, I wonder what the relationship will be like between my own three kids as they grow. What will they remember most from their childhood days and what will easily be forgotten along the way? Will they have similar interests or become polar opposites? Will they share the same values and morals that we hope to have taught them? Will they even be friends? Too often, I've heard stories where siblings don't speak; lack of communication, hard feelings from past experiences, or family history that's too dark to even try to brighten. Obviously, my husband and I hope for the best. As much as my kids may not want to admit it, they are each others' buddies. Underneath the bickering for toys, T.V., and territory, there is love.

When I reflect on my relationship with my sisters and sister-in-law, I recognize that they are the first people I turn to when I'm in a pickle. The primary people I trust to care for my children. I can always count on them. Family is family, plain and simple. As an adolescent and young adult, I didn't appreciate that. I got consumed with my daily life, friendships, boyfriends, after-school activities, and somehow my sisters got forgotten. Age differences, conflicting interests, and varying stages of life usually created the dividing forces between us. But somewhere along the road, when nieces and nephews started arriving and the pace of my life slowed down a bit, I began to realize just how important these relationships are.

Whenever I take an out-of-town vacation with my family, there is something comforting about coming home. Not just the physical structure of my home, but rather the true essence of the word. It's a feeling. My sisters are a part of that sense. We each have our own interpretation of the home we grew up in. We are connected to the memories and quite impressed by the resilience of our family tree. Like the giant maple that stands on their front lawn, my parents have weathered the storms, provided comfort when needed, and have always been there to lean on. While the tree has grown older, so have we. The branches have extended outward, providing shade on hot summer days and showcasing the beautiful colors of their leaves in autumn. It even holds the illuminated Christmas lights in order to spread the holiday cheer. Although, after my father fell while decorating one year, I am hesitant to admit, I think those lights stay set on those branches all year long.

I am, of course, ever grateful to "the tree" known as Mary Jane and David Boucher. They are the constant, whose roots I have grown to appreciate. But I am equally thankful for those two branches named Sharon and Bethany—my sisters. Sometimes I am frightened to grow up, but it is through the safe connections of family that I am reminded that I'll be okay.

17.
Inhale

Inhale. What a simple concept. Exhale, how easy! Yet, at times, why do I feel as though I am gasping for air, unable to exhale and inhale with a normal rhythm? I have battled with bouts of anxiety at certain times in my life. This feeling of panic that drapes over me, disabling my body from carrying out its simple tasks, is frightful! Thank God it's not typical. Usually, my panic manifests around medical issues. Dental visits, technicians drawing my blood (big trouble), the third trimester of pregnancy (when I had a full-blown belly and was unable to physiologically get an adequate breath of air), and very small spaces all evoke feelings of anxiety. Luckily, I have been able to keep it mentally under control, but I know it's somewhere, hidden below the surface.

Anxiety reminds me of a slithery reptile, snaking its way up my spine. When placed in a challenging situation and the feelings of anxiety arrive, my body immediately ignites reaction mode and reminds me that I need to be afraid. Once my brain receives this message, all deals are off, and so begins my fright that I might pass out. I pray that it won't happen, and then, the more I try to stop thinking about it, the more I can't control it. Before long, I'm down on the deck. Help! The mind is a powerful thing. It's just astonishing how dynamic it is. When anxiety wraps itself around me, I must find my quiet breath, seek calm, and attempt to knock out the nervousness. I am safe. Easier said than done. (Did someone just say "doctor"?)

Recently, I was faced with the harsh reality that my years of chewing gum and munching lots of candy have taken its toll on my teeth. As a child, eight of my molars were filled because each had developed a cavity. So much for good oral hygiene! With passing time, the maintenance phase of adulthood has started. Regrettably, I cracked a molar and it was in need of repair. Oh fudge! Let's just say, I was in search of my inner peace on the day I had to go in for the dental procedure. I was informed it would take two and a half hours. Trying to keep my mind at ease was a personal battle I fortunately was able to win. It started with my breathing. Each time I felt myself tightening up and leaning towards the darker side of panic, I took a deep breath in through the nose and then slowly exhaled. I needed to remain calm and release those heebie-jeebies.

Towards the end of the ordeal, I kept trying to focus my thoughts on funny events and smiling faces. I literally visualized Boss Hogg zipping around town on a Segway. Nothing like a little *Dukes of Hazard* to bring me some comic relief. I was desperate! It's interesting to realize how quickly life changes when suddenly I must pause from the daily rush and prepare myself mentally for an unpleasant encounter. In my mind, the hustle and bustle of action occurring outside the doctor's office curiously plays out in slow motion.

I'm convinced that all humans have some sort of hidden quirk. Ugly toes and a touch of anxiety are mine. Since my toes would require some sort of surgical procedure to be corrected, and medical issues make me nervous, I guess I'm stuck with both. Once we admit we all have something that sparks unwanted emotions, we must find a way to deal with the triggers. We can't let the fear swallow us up. The obstacles that get placed in front of us can be daunting, and obviously some issues are bigger and much more challenging than others. If we agree to acknowledge the problems and work at a plan to get through it, we can then celebrate the mental victories as they occur.

It was my mother's voice on the morning of my dentist appointment that provided me the comfort I needed. She reminded me of a saying she had heard years ago: "Faith is the bird that sings when the dawn is still dark." Simply interpreted, the bird knows that the sun will rise, so it begins to whistle its sweet songs. The bird doesn't hope or wonder if it will rise, it knows! I have to know I am okay. Not hope it, not wish it, but know it. She assured me I was fine, everything was all set, and not to worry. When I hung up the phone, my eyes immediately filled with tears (again). She's the one—the gift, the person who completely cares and understands my total psychological make-up.

With a half hour to go, as I lay in the chair staring out the window, I spotted a hawk soaring off in the distance. It was at that instant I knew I was home free. Whenever I see a hawk or a deer, I feel they have come to share some sort of life-affirming message. Call me crazy, but there is something spiritual about their presence. Living in Rhode Island, it is not uncommon to see hawks in the sky. Recognizing I may have been grasping at straws, it could have been a woodchuck or any other woodland vermin for all I cared; I was still reassured by its presence and its decision to be seen for a few brief seconds outside the dentist's office window. Later, on the retell to my mother, she interpreted the sighting as herself (disguised as the hawk) reminding me I was safe. In any case, that hawk in the distance signified some level of serenity and provided a sense of assurance that I needed.

There are moments in parenting when we experience the horrible close-call situations that could have happened, but thankfully did not: a toddler running towards traffic, a child somehow gets lost in a mall, or a son that escapes our viewpoint at the beach and has wandered away towards the sea of bathing suits and beach blankets. *What if the car didn't stop? What if they got kidnapped? What if they went towards the water?* How fast those episodes can horrify us. Those dreadful "What if?" moments can add years to a mother's birth age. The fact that we are able to even breathe at the end of some days will always remain a mystery; our resilience for emotional stains is unmatched.

So much of our stint as mother revolves around uncertainty. I realized with the birth of my first child that we mothers must be pre-wired to worry. I spoke at length with my own mother about her mother's nervousness as a parent. She questioned why *her* mother worried so much. She claimed that it wasn't until she became a mother herself that she could fully appreciate and understand how all-consuming the job of motherhood is. With the birth of my three children, I, too, agonize about their well-being at all times. I guess that's part of the job description.

Fortunately, I haven't experienced true pain. All of the "What ifs?" have been resolved with a "Thank God!" How awful for someone who has experienced the internal bruising and endless heartache of losing a loved one; how terribly sad to say goodbye. It must be a daily challenge to try not to lose oneself in the tears. Even when the sun is shining its goodness down, the inner feelings of sorrow must be too hideous to ignore.

Without question, parenthood challenges us to stay, even when we sense we should run—fast! There are definite days I see the asylum waiting off in the distance and wonder if it's time to mentally check in, yet the overall tone of our happiness starts with us. If we are constantly looking outward for joy, try taking a peek inside. We may surprise ourselves. As often as possible, try to take time to breathe and relish in those cute faces we have brought into this world. Some moments we hope are briefer than others, of course, but the tender times must be marveled at with a certain level of pride. Exhale.

18.
Mental Medicine

Have I completely lost my mind? After a long conversation with my friend Danika about how much I enjoyed practicing yoga a few years ago, we concluded it would be next to impossible to fit a class into the weeknight schedule. With her husband working most evenings and my husband involved in coaching and other after-school commitments, we determined the only way it would get done is if it were scheduled at 6:00 a.m. on a Saturday morning. Oof!

Not only was winter on its way, but the darkness the morning presents mixed with the bitter-cold temperatures of a Rhode Island winter made for a challenging combination. Nonetheless, feeling a pull towards my inner Ohm, I contacted the local yoga instructor and pitched my idea of a private session. She accepted, and with that, our Saturday morning ritual began. Six of my friends agreed to try it out. They were all yoga virgins. Once we started, we all became easily hooked. Perhaps "easily" is not the best term, but regardless, it became a routine that we all thoroughly enjoyed.

Wake up, sleepy head. The buzzer sounds. I struggle to adjust my eyes towards the clock and reluctantly rise from my cozy nest. My family members are sleeping . . . *all in my bed,* therefore, I must lumber through the dark room in silence. With my arms fully outstretched like Frankenstein so I don't walk into a wall, I feel for my workout clothes. Most of the time, I grab the appropriate clothing, but it is not uncommon to mistakenly pick up a pair of shorts when I actually think I am holding a shirt—there must be a better way.

Anyway, once I've gathered my gear, I grab my keys and walk out into the frigid pre-dawn air. I'm somewhat confused. Is it morning or night? I sit completely hunched forward in my car, waiting for the heat to start blowing some warmth my way. Often at this hour, the choices for good music on the radio are limited—a possible gospel reading or inspirational local talk show. Amen for the iPod. Once that music gets cranking, my body begins to wake. My headlights are completely off as I quietly pull out of my driveway. I feel like the pilot of a stealth bomber on a secret mission for inner peace.

As exhausted as I am to get out of that bed, the feeling I get when all is said and done is worth every minute. We sweat our guts off and are challenged both physically and mentally, but when the class has ended and we all lay still in Shavasana (the final relaxation stage of the session), in some small way I feel empowered to conquer the day—at least temporarily. To be submerged into relaxation in the company of six fine friends is quite nice.

Motherhood unlocks a universal understanding: same team, same goal—a happy, healthy baby. But what about the happy, healthy mommy? Where is she in the mix? We all have a story. Fill in the details a bit differently, change the names, faces, and actual experiences, but our familiar thread of motherhood is there.

With so many snags in our day, it's natural to question if we are happy with where we are in our lives. As we know, the daily dance of motherhood can get hurried, so it's important to take care of ourselves physically and try to get some exercise. This is a gentle nudge that has nothing to do with our athletic ability or our need to put down the fork full of Kung Pao Chicken. I'm referring to the "mental medicine" exercise provides for our brain. I do believe in the important correlation of body, mind, and mood. There is a connection, a vital connection to our overall enjoyment in life!

Taking care of oneself physically is by no means being selfish; in fact, quite the opposite. The six of us that set our alarm clocks for 5:20 a.m. so we don't miss out on any part of the daily routine are not doing this because we're self-centered. We're doing it because we deserve a moment of peace. We owe it to ourselves to be alone with friends, and we understand the positive effect this exercise has on our mood and overall enjoyment of the day ahead. It's not easy. It takes commitment. It's a choice. Take care of "you" first, and the rest will follow. Some days are harder than others, and I am thankful for my pals that are along for the ride.

A large portion of this book has been focused on our children, family, friendships, and the endless obligations of life. Now it is time for the spotlight to shine down on you, the happy, healthy mommy. Where is Richard Simmons when I need him? Heck, if that guy wearing satin shorts and a tank top bejeweled in Swarovski crystal can inspire a roomful of blue hairs to kick like Bruce Lee and air box like Marvelous Marvin Hagler, just imagine the energy he could bring our way.

Seriously though, let's pledge to live the life we want. Everyone wants to be healthy, whether we admit that or not. Nothing "tastes" better than putting on an old pair of jeans that were once too tight and now find they're resting loosely at our hips . . . *that tastes good . . . real good!* The mere thought of starting an exercise program can be daunting, though. It's a process. I will admit, I don't always love the "doing it" phase of exercise, but the "I'm finished" phase feels pretty darn sweet.

There are a million excuses not to do it, but if not now, when will it be more convenient? Next week? Next month? Maybe after the next baby? If I were told by a doctor that my child needed a half hour of medical attention each day, I would find the time to do it, no matter how crazy my schedule. If my child's teacher suggested she needed extra help in mathematics, I would somehow squeak in a chunk of time in order to provide homework support. Think of all the activities we willingly sign our kids up for, so why not find thirty minutes for ourselves?

Although yoga is a treat, running is my exercise of choice. It's free, my mind is cleared, I am connected to my thoughts, and an overall release of existing annoyances is accomplished. My friend Claire and I have been running at the crack of dawn for a while now. It's a struggle to resist my rational mind telling me to stay in bed, but I know that once we take our first step forward, the chitchatting therapy begins and soon we will be smiling. Make no bones about it, with noise levels comparable to front row seats at a Guns N Roses concert, it is a treat to temporarily escape the madness of home life. Some days we have to slow down because we may be cramped, tired, or too involved in a story that can't be described at such a fast clip. Other days, we fly right along. The distance, duration, or intensity is not the point of importance. What matters most is we are out there, we are moving, and surprisingly enough, we are laughing. This is mental medicine. Try it!

Whatever time of day and however I can fit it in, I try to make physical activity a part of my daily routine. Yet, with three kids and a full-time teaching job, that doesn't always happen. To be honest, I don't ever actually have the time to exercise, and sometimes I actually don't want to, either. But I always try to make the time. Nike said it best: "Just do it." When I take care of myself, I'm bringing a better self to the table.

Most recently, I had the opportunity to play on a woman's indoor soccer team ("Ladies of the 80s"). Many games were played at 9:00 p.m., and some were even as late as 11:00 p.m. A bit ridiculous, but fun once I got there. Putting on those shin pads was like readying myself for battle. Even though I am aging and certainly not a teen anymore, it was neat to get out there and play. Not to mention, the chance to get away from my house for an hour, once a week, was an obvious perk, too. If possible, seek out some athletic/exercise programs available locally to women. All levels and all abilities are usually offered.

So, eat the creamy ice cream. Why not? I remember years ago craving Ben & Jerry's so badly that I pulled into a convenience store and purchased a pint of Special Edition: Peanut Butter and Jelly ice cream—heavenly! I couldn't possibly wait until I got home. Desperate, with no spoon in the car, I dug my front teeth right into the pint. Life needs its palpable pleasures, but I don't advise doing this. Not only was it very chilly on my front choppers, it was surely an ugly sight for any drivers passing by on the roadway. But, hey, life is meant to be enjoyed. I saw a bumper sticker that read, "Beer is proof that God wants us to have fun!" and the same goes for yummy treats.

Often we look to celebrities and other icons for inspiration. Why not look to ourselves? Let's inspire ourselves to believe that with all we have accomplished as a mother, friend, wife, daughter, sister, or colleague, we owe it to ourselves to make it happen. Think of how patient we are with our kids, and yet we lose patience with ourselves so easily. Imagine the amount of daily praise we shower our children with, and yet we constantly criticize ourselves and distort our own self-image. Would we ever consider doing that to our children? Not a chance.

The challenge is difficult, but we can do this. Everyone benefits from a daily dose of mental medicine—not for pounds lost, but rather for sanity saved! Don't forget, happy Mommy, you are absolutely worth it. Do it for you. Ready, set, go for it!

19.
Mommy's Mission:
To Love and Lecture

I am convinced that the essential element of a positive parental game plan is love. I trust that as long as our children know they are loved, in every sense of the word, they will most definitely be okay. It is, after all, a mother's love that creates the ultimate foundation for her child. From there, the inner spirit of that individual can take shape. Each child will be faced with challenges, but as long as that base of support is solid and trusted, the challenges will be met with greater success.

Kids secretly love to be acknowledged by their parents, although most would not admit it. My mother always spoke highly of me around others and she was not shy to gush of my accomplishments, either. It could become quite embarrassing at times because I am not a person that likes to boast. But, I must admit, it always felt nice to know that she was proud of me. Kids want to see our smile and realize that they are the contributing factor for it being on our face. These little miracles are difficult to figure out, though—even impossible at times. Just when they finish pushing us away, they want to pull us right back in.

One of the best gifts I can give my own three kids is consistency: consistent love, consistent follow-through, and consistent recognition for the jobs well done. Checking homework daily, addressing behavioral issues, and setting a predictable bedtime routine all provide a dependable schedule where my children know what to expect. This practice is helpful, but shouldn't be confused with rigidity. As we all know, schedules change, so if my kids aren't in bed until 10:30 p.m. on a summer night, don't notify DCYF. But be mindful, we are the model, the exemplar of sorts. We're not flawless, but we must be savvy enough to recognize that kids process our every move. They are watching, and when we least expect it, those listening ears are tuned in, absorbing each juicy detail like a dried-up sponge. I witness this at school. If a student misbehaves in class, many children will immediately look at me to observe my reaction. Kids are aware.

Years ago, I had a student approach me and say, "Mrs. Carr, I never see you mad or upset." I chuckled and then replied, "If that statement is true, consider yourself lucky. You must have been in a class where the children cooperated, respected one another, and simply got the job done." In my P.E. classes, I do get upset when someone is mistreated or disrespected. I am bothered by people who choose to cheat or act sneaky because I spend a lot of time encouraging kids to be cooperative with their classmates.

In my early years of teaching, I had a student who got busted for cheating on the half-mile run. When I called him over to question his performance, he immediately burst into tears. Complaining about the pain caused by his shoes, he couldn't get the complete story straight. Was it really the feet or was he embarrassed that he got caught? I think the latter. Once I reassured him that he could sit down and re-test on another day, the foot pain mysteriously vanished. Within minutes, he was ready to participate in the next activity: Ninja Turtle Tag . . . Hmm, very interesting.

My question is, on the retell to his parents, would the accurate details of the occurrence be told or would some of the specific details be changed? Delete the cheating part and focus only on those aching feet? That little boy was a real cute kid, but when faced with the fact he may have been beaten by someone else, he panicked. Talk to those kiddies and listen to their concerns—really listen! But realize, though, that some of the details may not necessarily be factual.

Take, for example, the year I was engaged to be married. Somehow the fact that Andy was also a P.E. teacher had come up in conversation with a parent from school. She thought it was neat that my fiancé was in the same profession. She went on to say how much the kids at his school really enjoyed him as a teacher and how convenient that we both taught in the same school district. That's when the light bulb went off in my head. I realized she had Andy confused with someone else, because we do not teach in the same town. I stopped her and asked who she thought I was marrying. She named the P.E. teacher at the other elementary school in my district. I said, "No, I am not marrying him. I'm marrying Andy Carr." She was absolutely shocked! She couldn't believe it. So much talk had been going on during the car-pool rides to and from her daughter's basketball practices, she was certain it could only be the truth. Like a classic game of telephone, once the story was passed between a few listeners, the original facts got lost in the shuffle. I recognize this same type of miscommunication at school.

Occasionally in class, someone will report that a fellow chum has used a certain *bad word*. The serious messenger will often make reference to the use of the "S" word or sometimes it could even be as bad as the "D" word. Imagine my disbelief, when approached, because my students range in ages of five to nine years old. When I press the student for more information regarding the actual word in question, I often have to restrain myself from laughing. The "S" word usually means "stupid" and the "D" word often stands for "dumb." How refreshing! We adults certainly have much saltier definitions for those "S" and "D" words, but I love that youthful innocence.

However, last year that amusing sweetness regrettably got tainted. I had two kids run up to me and say, "Mrs. Carr, come quick! We have to show you something really bad!" I was nervous so I moved swiftly. When they brought me to the scene of the horror, the two boys apprehensively pointed to the floor. Right there in black ink were the words, "Mrs. Carr stinks ass." Obviously, I had annoyed someone with my rules of kindness and equality, but, oddly enough, it actually made me laugh. At the time, as a parent of a two-year-old, I did indeed "stink ass" each time I had to change my daughter's diaper. So in some strange way that angry student was literally correct.

We all know how painfully honest children can be. It is not uncommon to hear a young child say exactly what comes to their mind in a quite unpredictable situation. For some reason, shopping excursions can bring out the best of embarrassing moments for parents. One morning Jane and I were in the

greeting card section of a store. While I looked for a card, Jane
had her eyes set on other sights. One in particular was a woman
about eighty-eight years old. "Is she a grandma?" she asked. "I
don't know, why do you ask?" I replied. Jane continued,
"*It* looks old. *It* has silver hair." Good thing "*It*" didn't
hear her because I'm sure that doesn't provide a big
boost to the overall self-esteem. I remember waiting
in line at a ticket booth at a traveling carnival and
hearing a young child shout, "Look, that man has
a tattoo on his neck!" only to find out this person
wearing the bolo tie and a Marlboro belt buckle was,
in fact, a woman and she was definitely not amused.
I particularly enjoyed the memorable moment my
child pointed to the aging war veteran wearing an
eye patch and yelled, "Look, Mommy, it's Jack
Sparrow." Boy, was I proud. Those comments are
always dynamite to hear coming from a child's mouth. Often
in those embarrassing instants I take on traits of Helen Keller
and pretend to not see or hear what my child just said. Rather,
I give the "you are in big trouble" glare and save the follow-up
discussion to address the rudeness for later.

My mission as Mommy has a purpose, with respect, dignity,
and honor as top priorities. As parents, we are all important
messengers in the emotional classroom of life. Be a pioneer, set
the standards high, and don't hesitate to facilitate the nitty-gritty
lessons that kids need to learn. It's critical. The assignments are
everlasting, thus making our job as teacher limitless. Kids have
the power to achieve greatness, and with the right people in
their corner, they will.

20.
Parent as Spectator

When watching my children engage in activities with friends, I hope they will never be bullied and by no means be made to feel sad. As they swim through society, sometimes like a fish out of water, my only wish is that they experience the least amount of pain as possible. Life as a parent looking in from the outside is torturous at times. Somehow, it seemed easier as the kid. I always felt I had control of the situation even when I absolutely did not!

As the parent, all control is forfeited as I wait and observe my children try to flourish on this giant spinning sphere. Sometimes they'll go down, sometimes they'll prevail. Oftentimes they'll surprise me and unfortunately they'll upset me. They will be pushed, shoved, pinched, and scratched, but because they are human, those accidents always seem to heal, thanks to the natural phenomenon known as the anatomy of life.

Witnessing those moments of immediate physical pain, I pray that their emotional chemistry won't be affected to the same extent. I disagree with that old phrase, "sticks and stones may break my bones, but names will never hurt me." Verbal teasing and being made fun of hurts more than the occasional bump, bang, or playground punch. A black eye on the face heals much quicker than a black eye on the soul. No question.

We imagine our children as they hop on the school bus for the first time. Off they go, leaving the nest. We picture the scene at school. *Will they have someone to sit with at lunchtime? Who will they play with at recess? Will they be liked? Are they nervous?* The role of "parent as spectator" is difficult. Take a drive by an elementary school playground. The scene of children swinging, the sounds of laughter, and the sight of constant moving bodies are quite sweet. The view from the car, with windows rolled up, paints such an innocent picture. But sometimes, if we turn off the car's engine, roll down the windows, and tune up those listening ears, we may experience a different feel. The sounds of laughter can change quickly to echoes of anger, teasing, or torment. Life on a playground is not easy. It is survival of the fittest and kids can be cruel. It's such a joy to witness kids being childlike, but acting childish is a different story. The laughter, enthusiasm, excitement, and innocence are refreshing. The childish stuff is annoying: whining, pouting, and quitting. That type of behavior is sure to get a negative response.

When I was playing on the tennis team in high school, I encountered a childish opponent three years in a row. We both played number one singles, matching up against each other every fall. In the game of tennis, the players are responsible for honestly calling their own shots; a sport based on dignity and trust. This girl consistently made questionable line calls as to whether or not the ball was in or out.

She was clearly the better player, but during one particular match I had miraculously pulled ahead and was now leading in the set. It was time to switch sides of the court. At that moment, she walked towards the net, sat down, cradled her knees with her arms, and rocked back and forth, chanting, "I'm not going to lose this match," repeatedly for three minutes, until the drink break was over; kind of creepy, a bit scary, but most of all, very sad. Was she having fun? This childish behavior resembled a young girl who wanted to stomp her feet and take her toys home. When she finally resumed her ability to play, she immediately called the next point "Out!" My mother (as spectator) cheered that I had won the point, which was clearly "in"; the girl then turned to my mother and said, in a rather condescending tone, "That ball was out!" Well, that was all MJ needed to send mother lion into action. My mother had observed this player's unsportsmanlike conduct too many times, now she was pissed.

From across the court, I spotted my mother's face—eyes glaring, teeth clenched, and rising up from behind her can of Tab . . . What was that I saw? . . . Could it be? MJ had conspicuously raised her middle finger (for only my eyes to see), as if to say, "Go get her, Chris! Don't take that crap." Ha! I had never seen that side of my mother before. It was shocking, but so appreciated. This was the former PTO President and Girl Scout Troop Leader now asserting her own inner fire. I loved it! It was exactly what I needed to spark my adrenaline and finish the match with a victory. Faced with a potential defeat, that girl began to unravel. As a result, she looked to the childish choices of cheating, complaining, and mental breakdown. Unfortunately, her coach did not address any of these undesirable traits and allowed the inexplicable performance to continue.

As my children age and develop interest in athletics, music, drama, or any other recreational activity, I hope they will be blessed with effective coaches. A good coach challenges people to rise above. They demand effort, hard work, and emphasize positive character traits.

I used to coach girls' middle school basketball and softball. As the Varsity coach of that program, there was only one team—no junior varsity. Therefore, that gave me the dreaded responsibility of conducting try-outs and making cuts. How is it possible to take thirty athletes and make up a basketball team of sixteen without hurt feelings, sadness, and regret?

Each year, after four days of practice drills, physical endurance challenges, and continued evaluations, I would choose the team. It was never easy to do. Some girls would be thrilled and others would be left disheartened. Every time the "cutting" process occurred, I felt sad. To exclude someone from anything and cast them aside goes against my entire belief system. I always wished that someone else could take over that responsibility: pick ten great players, and then let me step in to take charge. But that wasn't the case.

One year, I received a phone call at school the day after basketball cuts were made. This was no ordinary phone call. The woman on the other end was livid and rightfully so. Her daughter had been cut from the team and she wanted answers. After all, this was her child. The girl she watched shooting hoops in her driveway, the daughter she carted around to recreational games, practices, and summer camps. She began with, "Who the hell do you think you are? You have ruined my daughter's self-esteem . . ." I assured her that I would be willing to meet and go over the entire collection of data I recorded from her daughter's try-out. She agreed, but I wouldn't be meeting with her, she was sending her husband instead. Oh boy!

The next day, our school secretary poked her head into the gym and informed me of his arrival. Oh shit! My heart rate skyrocketed as if I were sprinting on a treadmill. I wished I was a child again, giggling with my friends without a care in the world. If only I could hide. Well, obviously that wasn't an option and soon enough the children filed out and the irate father walked in. Wait a minute. Much to my surprise, he was not carrying a fiery torch and he, indeed, was not masked in leather. Rather, this man wore a kind smile and offered an outstretched hand. I introduced myself and waited for the bomb to hit. It never did. This father calmly began by explaining that he has always stressed the importance of hard work and determination with his daughter. He believed that if there was something to be improved upon, he wanted to know what could be done. How could his young seventh grader better her basketball abilities? What were her strengths and what were her weaknesses? What did she need to do in order to improve?

The girl's parents were an important ingredient to this story. The father was obviously calmer after having time to process the situation, whereas "mother bear" was much more fired-up. They were both naturally upset, but after honest discussion and open communication, they recognized what needed to be worked on in order for their daughter to improve her skill level. They provided the emotional support and stood by their daughter to hug away the heartache associated with feeling bad. But, unfortunately, the girl had to experience the situation herself. With the loving support of her parents and the teachable moments they brought to the table, that young girl clearly became a contributing player in the years to come for her high school team. She didn't quit, she didn't make excuses, but instead proved to herself that she absolutely could do it.

Up to this point, I've known every bump, bruise, triumph, and struggle that my children have experienced. The small bundles I cradled so gently in my arms as babies will continue to execute their performances while I wait calmly in the wings. Yeah, right. Good parents give their children the strength to cope, but part of the job is letting go. Kids hold our hands through all of the aches and pains, yet one day they'll release their grip.

We recognize that the job of parent as spectator is complicated. When it comes to our own children, it's personal! As years pass, the daily details will fade from my memory. It's not always easy to watch. Whether it's ballpark bullying or struggles with social connections, mothers feel their child's sadness. They sense it—a mother always knows! We all want our kids to belong, to be liked, and to be accepted. As parents, we can chart the course through these younger years, but it is our child who one day will raise the sail and venture forth. While we stand back, clutching the safety vest if needed, we hope they'll continue to always coast smoothly with the cautious currents of life.

21.
Maternal Expressway

I have always been someone who races to get places. Before children, the pace was fast but there was always time to rest and recover. However, this maternal race I speak of is a whole different beast.

While I administered Jane her antibiotic for an ear infection, packed the lunches for the day, checked around the house for Nolan's library books, wrote a return message to his teacher, wiped down the counters, cleared away the breakfast dishes, and then unclogged a toilet that was jammed with an overabundance of toilet paper (Finleeeeyyyyy!), it hit me. Shockingly, it wasn't even 7:30 a.m. yet, and my day was just revving up.

My sister Beth was coming over early that morning (she watches the children four days a week, while my sister-in-law has them on Wednesdays). This particular day, she would get Nolan on the bus so that I could drop my car off to be serviced. The driver's side window was sticking and making some rather disturbing sounds when I rolled it down. With temperatures dipping into the low 20s, it would be just my luck for it to break at the next drive-thru and not be able to roll back up.

I wasn't going to work that day. Not only was my car getting taken care of, I had a scheduled root canal for 9:45 a.m., as well. I recognize the insanity of this and laugh. With all of the morning tasks to be taken care of, who has time for personal pain when we're the mommy?

I wish I could say I was making this scenario up, but remarkably enough, this is a glimpse of the somewhat average *start* to a day in the life of motherhood. Help! And forget about what happens as the day progresses. Normally, I must hightail it home from work to pick up Finley, grab Jane from her pre-school, and then zip back to my house in order to get Nolan off the bus. But make no bones about it; the day doesn't end there. As we all know, a whole new responsibility begins when that big yellow bus comes barreling up the roadway!

What is up with this round-the-clock activity? We all know the stories of Tommy getting picked up from gymnastics and being rushed immediately to Tae Kwan Do, or Susie leaving dance class early in order to make it to her swim lesson . . . Ahhhhhh! Are we having fun yet? Do the kids even know where the hell they are? Sports participation is a wonderful part of life, but whatever happened to one sport per season? In graduate school, I based my entire master's thesis project on the concept of over-scheduling our youth and how it related to the eventual burnout for some individuals. We need to be careful because all of this extra-curricular activity has quietly become a parent-driven force, instead of a child-driven desire.

When I was younger, my parents paid a $20 registration fee for the entire softball or basketball season. The games were played locally around the city at various fields and gymnasiums. There were no hitting clinics, batting practices, or basketball skills training. There were no year-long commitments, either.

No travel teams and no private lessons. If our team had to travel, it was because we had won the local division and had moved on to the regional or national tournament. Later on in high school, I conveniently switched from one season to the next without even batting an eyelash at the sport that just passed.

Nowadays, it feels like a constant internal chase. The endless rush from place to place, always glancing at the clock, hoping I'll get to that next engagement *on time*. The intensity of this job is exhausting! Who is going where? Do you need a ride? Where is the birthday party? What time does it start? Did we get the gift? As I hustle, bustle, nag, and hurry, many times I wonder if I'm the only mother not finding this fun.

Take a look at the cars driving by on the road. Sneak a peek at the fogged-over faces, the blank stares, and the white-knuckled grips on the wheel. Where are we all going? Check to see if there are car seats in the back. If so, are those seats occupied by little bodies? Maybe the mom is taking her cherubs on the "$25.00 nap ride." She doesn't care what the price of gasoline is, as long as that baby is sleeping—drive, baby, drive!

The women at the wheel know this story. We are living it each day. The noises from inside are muted, but we understand a little of what's going on in their thoughts. "Mommy, pass me my sippy cup . . . it fell," or "Mommy, she hit me," or "Play that Barney song again; and again, and again, and again." Fast forward to the adolescent years: "Mom, this music sucks, change the station," or "Mom, by the way, when my friends get in the car, don't talk," or "Mom, drop me off at the corner so no one can see you." Ah, more perks of motherhood.

Wouldn't it be nice to see that hypothetical black and white checkered flag waving in the wind as we arrived to our driveway? A symbol confirming that the sprint has ended. Unfortunately, we're smart enough to realize that the race never ends. It will start right back up in the morning, or possibly in the middle of the night, for some.

How do we maintain the family traditions when we are constantly rushing to the next task? As a kid, I consistently ate dinner with my family at the dining room table and my mother said, "Good night, God bless you, pleasant dreams, I love you," every night . . . just before she reached for the Scotch. She wrote a note on my lunch napkin each day when I went to school. Yet, as I got a little older, I had to put an end to it (it's not so cool at the junior high level to read love notes from Mommy).

I realize that there will be much more fun ahead—the teen years, boyfriends and girlfriends, cell phones, text messaging, and spendy wardrobes. "Where are the keys?" will be demanded from a young driver wanting to use our car, heated arguments with siblings will occur, and hormonal peaks and plunges will be experienced. They will, no doubt, master the skill necessary to answer, "I don't know," to every question a parent will ask, they'll most likely acquire the keen ability to restrain from giving parents any specific details of their daily adventures, and super sweet comments such as, "I hate this house," or "You're not like Mary's mom, you're mean!" will probably be voiced as well. During those jolly-good times, I'll be wishing for the challenges that involved who gets to play with the Star Wars figures and whether to watch PBS or Cartoon Network.

One night, after an evening of jam-packed fun, I reached my breaking point of parental frustration and began to bawl my eyes out—sobs, snorts, and all. This display of emotion was the result of my child's "what's next?" mentality. I recognized that it didn't matter what I did yesterday, three weeks ago, or even ten minutes ago, at that. I could take my kids to the toy shop, stop for a nice lunch, meet friends at the local playground, and then go to a movie. But as soon as the fun bus returns home to reality, all deals are off. Within minutes, I hear, "I'm bored." Realistically, I am doing more with my kids in one day than my mother did with us in a whole month—and she was a great mom! While I stand twirling a baton of choices, I wonder how much fun is necessary. And do our kids even care?

Quite clearly, we're doing it all. We all need support. We are skilled and able, but the reality is we can certainly benefit from assistance. The acceptance of help from others should be appreciated willingly. Luckily, my in-laws have provided hours of loving care for our three children when Andy and I have had the chance to go out on a "date." Now and then, we have had to seek help from outside the family ties. The criteria for acceptable qualifications have certainly changed over the years. When we first left our son home alone with a babysitter, the extensive list of concerns was carefully posted and reviewed with the caregiver, and step-by-step, detailed directions of the entire routine were explained. Heck, who am I kidding? Dr. Henry Heimlich's maneuver for choking was probably demonstrated and basic CPR techniques may have been discussed.

Three kids later and the expectations have undoubtedly been altered. The only questions we have now for the sitter are, "Do you have a pulse?" and "Are you capable of dialing 911?" Great, you'll be fine. Obviously only kidding, but sometimes parents get desperate. Not to mention, the list of tasks that need to be accomplished no longer exists. Just a cell phone number, a hug for each child, and "Have fun!" exclaimed from the car as we bake-tire out of the driveway. Free at last. Yee-ha!

As women, we live in a culture where we have a chance to choose. Some women of the world don't have that privilege. Elect the sunshine and limit the rain. If life is getting too busy and rushed, decelerate the engine and choose a different path. The most important thing about this daily race is the cast of characters in our care. As much as those passengers can test our patience, they're not always concerned about crossing the finish line. Sometimes they are simply enjoying the ride.

Then immediately put on that left blinker, get your ass back in the high-speed lane, and get moving. You'll never get there on time. Let's see that white-knuckled grip clutching the steering wheel! Oh fantastic, stuck behind another school bus. That's just great. *!%#*@! Beeeep!

22.
The Magical Moments

I can't help but recognize that family home videos manage to only capture the fabulous seasons of life—each child so perfectly innocent. Giant smiles blanket the faces of each participant and every person in view, surprisingly, looks happy. Very rarely are the cameras rolling for the true temper tantrums and emotional breakdowns. Those video clips that do show some memorable episodes of splendor are usually worthy of serious prize money on *America's Funniest Home Videos*—not exactly comical when the incident occurs, but not so bad if I can collect some cash for the annoyance.

The performance of life would be much easier if we could press pause when things got too scary, wait for the unflattering moments to pass, then easily resume filming once the confusion had cleared. But we all know that's impossible. Each day is not recordable. It is a treat, however, to reflect in awe on our life. It's astonishing to realize that those little wonders who create the very beautiful memories can also cause the most tiresome episodes of all.

Recently, my family viewed video clips from my parents' wedding day. I tried to focus in on the traditional moments of the reception: the father/daughter and mother/son dances, in particular. During both parts of the video, I became teary-eyed. That adoring look a mother gives to her son and that heartfelt emotion expressed through the look in a father's eyes just made my heart sad. Are they remembering the aggravations of the day-to-day routine or are they simply enjoying the moment? I think we all know the answer to that one. The twinkle in a mother's eye and the absolute beam of a father's face reflects the incredible love deep within. Those instances signify a journey shared between a family—so many days, so many memories.

It was also quite charming to see my parents in a stage of their life before all of "this" began—a blank slate so open for the additions of life. If they knew then what they know now, what would change? What would they hope to erase? And what has been of most importance and value? If the daily buzz was muted and only the beautiful faces were observed, it would be easy to forget the trials we go through. How quickly we can erase the negatives and hone in only on the highlights and positives. That's the beauty of family. We are willing to forget, forgive, and press on, concentrating only on the good we see in each other.

Not a day goes by that I don't acknowledge how truly blessed I am. One particular Mother's Day morning, while pretending to be asleep, I heard the sounds of my three little kiddies downstairs, each "quietly" trying to create a homemade card with Daddy.

"Where are the crayons?"

"Shhh!"

"Oops!"

"Who knocked over the flowers?"

How innocent and unrehearsed. The fact that they honestly believed I was still sleeping and completely surprised was priceless. I smile just thinking about it. Through all of the clamoring, clanging, and pots and pans crashing, I was actually able to fake that I was utterly shocked and oblivious—another precious moment for the memory book filed securely in my mind.

Unfortunately, though, not every moment is one for the scrapbooks. Often mothers do get stuck doing the lame jobs associated with parenting. The most recent irritation occurred when my daughter corked the drain to the bathroom sink, and then turned on the water. This genius idea created a flowing waterfall over the counter, onto the floor, and into 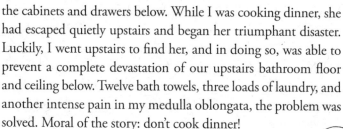 the cabinets and drawers below. While I was cooking dinner, she had escaped quietly upstairs and began her triumphant disaster. Luckily, I went upstairs to find her, and in doing so, was able to prevent a complete devastation of our upstairs bathroom floor and ceiling below. Twelve bath towels, three loads of laundry, and another intense pain in my medulla oblongata, the problem was solved. Moral of the story: don't cook dinner!

Mothers are usually so busy doing those "clean-ups" that we don't always get time to physically interact with our kids as much as we'd like. Sometimes we find ourselves caught up in the details of wanting everything to look perfect and be perfect, and we miss out on the little things. Then in walks Daddy, bearing balloons, Slushies, and demanding that they all share in a secret handshake. Short of donning a red, curly wig while dressed in a garment dappled with polka dots, he's "Good Time Gary" bringing home the fun. Suddenly, this brief, energized moment of activity becomes the highlight of our kid's day, while we moms stand exhausted in the background. Where is our secret handshake?

We women need to rise up and start our own little revolution. Instead of standing on the sidelines *watching* the fun, let's get down on the floor and *create it!* Truth be told, kids don't care how clean the house is and they don't care what's for dinner, so it's okay, at times, to let that stuff settle. Why not allow the kids to jump on the couches and bounce on the beds? Why can't we hop on the floor and wrestle the kids to the ground? How come we don't encourage chocolate bars for breakfast; dads get to do it, so why not us? Why do we always have to play the responsible role? *Quality vs. Quantity.* Mothers tend to worry about *how much* time we spend with our children instead of focusing on the *enjoyment* of the actual experience. Once a week, let's adopt a role reversal and enjoy the view from the floor.

Not too long ago, I was driving back from an out-of-town friend's house. The trip took just enough time for all of my kids to conk out on the ride home. When I glanced in my rear view mirror, I couldn't help but recognize just how cute they looked. I wished I had my camera; however, taking pictures while driving sixty miles an hour doesn't seem very practical. They reminded me of three little birds. Those blond little birds have a way of nesting right on my heart—comfy-cozy. Sometimes I get poked by a few twigs and branches, but the warmth of their feathers always prevails.

It would be so nice if only the recorded perfection occurred, but I do have to accept that a lot of action behind the scenes is what makes the whole experience so memorable. It's okay that everyone looks pretty in the picture, but it's also funny to remember that someone was getting pinched in the background. That is the true reality, and as complicated as it might be, I appreciate that the show must go on.

23.
In Life, Laughter Prevails!

Laughter is great medicine—the best! How healing it is. We need to do more of it. I love the honesty of friendship and the happiness that it brings. I am rewarded with companions who have showered my spirit with entertaining stories and helped me maintain my true, joyful self. Those special chums in my life who continue to make me beam are the true players in my daily game. Of course, my family is first, but without these connections, my life would surely be missing a part of its soul. These attachments have provided me with endless smiles, the deepest of emotions, and the tremendous laughter that make this adventure so much fun. I am forever indebted. Great friends are like air: they are vital to our existence, so breathe them in!

At thirty-seven, I can honestly say I have had a wonderful ride, but I am definitely not ready to get off. I am thankful for each day, good and bad. I remember wondering how sad my mother must have been after losing her parents. Why her? An only child, twenty-three years old, so full of life, kind and loving—beautiful, in every sense of the term—why did she have to experience such pain? Well, years later, I feel that through her sadness and loss she taught her three daughters how important it was to be strong. She was the strongest one of all. Through her life, we realized that we could do anything.

She is not perfect, nobody is. But, undeniably, we always trusted her love and with that understanding, we had the true power to be survivors.

It's natural for a busy mother to feel blinded in the early stages of motherhood. It's such a blow to our freedom and care-free social life. It comes back, an altered version, of course; we just have to be patient. When my son was in first grade, he made me a plant for Mother's Day. I commented on its beauty and he recounted the necessary elements that were needed to make his plant grow: soil, sun, space, water, and patience. The last part of the list was most important. How difficult it is to wait and allow things to take shape, especially when parenting our children. Like the seeds placed in the fresh soil, with proper nurturing and care, they will blossom. Little did I know that a simple Mother's Day project would remind me of such a valued virtue.

Like I said from the get-go, I don't pretend to have the correct answers. Without the necessary support team of friends and family, I'm busted. I learn everyday from these people, and certainly through the eyes of my three young children. Their lives are just getting started and I can't wait to watch them become their magical individual selves. No doubt, comments such as, "Mommy, my forth-head (forehead) hurts," will get replaced with much less amusing phrases. The childhood tea parties will end and Diego and Dora will no longer be the distinguished guests of honor. The messes they create will not easily be vacuumed away and the angelic sound of their voices will eventually drift away.

Keep in mind, this is a story based on the truth. We all want to be a fabulous mother, wife, friend, daughter, sister, coworker, etc. So let's just admit that we are magnificent creatures, accept our downfalls, and quiet the voices that keep telling us what to do next. The illusion that parenthood is going to be perfectly joyful is just that—an illusion. We know that every day is not going to be saturated with sugar and spice (we have to get the Frank's Red Hot in there sometimes), but if we allow ourselves to look for the brighter side of an issue, the darker times may not feel as gloomy. Occasionally, the pleasant sounds of innocent giggles and sweet baby voices get muffled by the many challenges that get thrown our way. As often as possible though, we must smother those little tots with love, listen to their laughter, and enjoy.

Many women before us paved this path of opportunity. Some would roll over in their graves to see where it got us. Their intentions were not to create a train wreck. We owe it to them and we owe it to ourselves to create a life that can be enjoyed; don't settle for one filled with frustration and sadness. We know full well how fortunate we are to declare the words, "That's my child!" It's such a telling statement. To be blessed with children is indeed a true miracle, but so is the notion that we actually make it through the day alive!

Whatever happens, I am convinced we need to wake up and put an end to some of the nonsense. We cannot possibly solve every problem for our children. Life on the imperfect playground is not easy; therefore, welcome the idea that some lessons have to be figured out on their own. It is usually through our challenges that we realize who we are and how well equipped we are to cope. Some of my best lessons were often learned from my biggest mistakes—trial and error. Also, we have to stop comparing ourselves to everyone else. Just as I tell my students in P.E. class, "compare yourself to yourself." That's it! Be the best that you can be, not what someone else can be.

So go ahead and pat yourself on the back. You are the gift, the absolute gift to your children and family. It's time to rise up, face the crowd, and take a bow; a virtual curtain call. You are admired and applauded. Your audience loves you. Stand proud! Continue to look for the laughter, even when it may seem impossible to find, and remember we only get one time around on this ride. Live life and live it well. There are little eyes watching, so be brilliant!

You
as Composer

This book has rested gently in the palms of your hands as you have read through the pages. Your fingerprints are everywhere (chocolate sauce and all). My sincere expectation is that you have laughed, remembered similar episodes of madness, and hopefully made some connections. Now it's time to truly make this book your own. Grab a pen and add stories from your personal treasure trove of experiences. It is through writing that we can usually alleviate some of the annoyances and solidify the beautiful flashes of life's many journeys. Write, cross out, scribble, jot down ideas, and enjoy the reflections!

Christine Carr has been an elementary school Physical Education teacher since 1993. A graduate of the University of Rhode Island, the author takes her many years of teaching experience and puts it front and center as it relates to the everyday occurrences associated with life as a parent.

Christine lives in South Kingstown, Rhode Island, with her husband, Andrew, and their three children. This is her first book. Enjoy!

Her web site is christine-carr.com